THE NEW BLACK URBAN ELITES

BY: WILL D. TATE

San Francisco, California
1976

Published in 1976 by
R and E Research Associates
4843 Mission Street, San Francisco 94112
18581 McFarland Avenue, Saratoga, California 95070

Publishers and Distributors of Ethnic Studies
Adam S. Eterovich
Robert D. Reed

Library of Congress Card Catalog Number

75-38301

ISBN

0-88247-394-8

TABLE OF CONTENTS

CDP.2

LIST OF TABLES

Chapter 1

THE OAKLAND BLACK MIDDLE CLASS

Marxist theorists have traditionally defined the bourgeoisie as a ruling class that controls the means of production. This class dominates the economic, political and social areas of society. The executive of a modern state is seen as a committee that manages the affairs of a modern state in the interest of the whole bourgeoisie. The bourgeoisie is not a stagnant class. Rather it is dynamic. It rose to its position of dominance by using revolutionary means and maintains its superiority by constantly adapting new means and techniques to production by manipulation of the masses. Marx viewed the landlords, shopkeepers and pawnbrokers as a portion of the bourgeoisie who participate in the oppression of the lower classes. Eventually portions of the bourgeoisie, ideologists and intellectuals join with the working classes in revolution against the bourgeoisie class and assist the proletariat in gaining control of their destinies politically, economically and socially.

Marxism has become attractive to many people of diverse backgrounds and racial heritages. It has spread in various forms to several continents and countries, from China to Burma to Ghana, Moscow to Belegrade and Djakarta. In each area that has accepted Marxism it was necessary to redefine some of the concepts of Marx's theories to meet the needs of the localized situation. Although there are certain universal characteristics of the antagonistic classes, each society is in a different state of modernity and the characteristics of the bourgeoisie tend to differ. These various societies usually maintain their own ideologist who constantly analyze Marxist theory in the light of their unique situations. It is to be expected in considering a model of internal colonialism, the concept of a bourgeoisie is redefined and this redefinition is dictated by realities of a different social and economic situation. The colonized antagonistic classes are influenced by the dynamics of colonization. In internal colonialism both the bourgeoisie and the working classes are colonized and the colonized bourgeoisie does not have direct control of the means of production or decisive political power.

Attempts to place the colonized elites into the Marxist model of a bourgeoisie is a herculan task indeed, given their lack of independent power and their inability to directly control the means of production. This picture is modified to some extent, when we consider their relationships to production and their roles as leaders in social mobilization and modernization. It is further modified when the elites' perceptions of their roles are considered. Marx allowed for different strata in the bourgeoisie and this further simplifies our conceptual problem. He included landlords, pawnbrokers and others in his definition of the bourgeoisie. They obviously had little direct control over the means of production. They were included so far as they participated in activities tangentially related to maintenance of the ruling classes at the expense of the proletariat. For Marx the lower middle class consisted of the small trades people: shopkeepers and the retired tradesmen.[1]

This study is based upon several premises embedded in the relations between Afro-Americans and the dominant white race. The first premise is that Afro-Americans generally, were colonized in Africa and transported to the New World by force. They were colonized in America, oppressed and forced into slavery. The direct domination of slavery evolved into a method of domination almost uniquely American. This new method had both assimilationist and indirect rule aspects. A degree of modernization of the black American population was permitted within certain limitations. The dynamics of oppression was accompanied by an internal colonial structure that is

1

different only in degree to traditional colonialism. Finally, all levels of the structure are functionally interrelated in the colonial model.

Analyzing any political or economic system whether capitalist or socialist is a very complicated exercise, especially when it is compounded by a theory of colonization. In this study only one segment of the structure is investigated-- the colonized black bourgeoisie of the Oakland, California area. Major historical, social and economic forces have been outlined to place the actors within a time frame, to point up the general social environment on a national level and to provide a context within which the respondents are acting.

The colonial model has several universal characteristics in both traditional and internal colonial situations. Among these characteristics are: domination by force directly or indirectly; a mother country that benefits psychologically, politically or economically from exploitation and at least three definable social and economic classes, the colonizer, the colonized elite and the colonized masses.

David E. Apter, in his study of patterns of indirect rule in colonial situations, placed the colonized elites into two groups. The traditional elites who were legitimized in various clusters such as family, the chieftaincy hierarchy, the state council (oman) and other membership structures.[2] Another elite group was established outside of the traditional authority framework that was based on skills and education. The latter group achieved their positions through selective recruitment by the colonizer and was trained in mission and foreign schools. They were given posts in the civil service or with European firms. There was often conflict between the two groups as to direction of action within the colony.[3]

Jean-Paul Sartre describes the method of establishing a new modernizing elite in the colonies as follows:

"The European elite undertook to manufacture a native elite. They picked out promising adolescents; they branded them, as with a red-hot iron, with principles of Western culture; they stuffed their mouths full with high-sounding phrases, grand glutinous words that stuck to the teeth. After a short stay in the mother country they were sent home, white-washed."[4]

In the colonial model the colonizer class is an instrument of oppression placed directly above the colonized bourgeoisie in the colonial hierarchy. Albert Memmi indicates the colonizers are the colonial administrators, military and petty bourgeoisie who exploit the colony in the name of the mother country.[5] Julian H. Steward indicates that in the United States and in many colonial areas mediating agents may include administrators, missionaries, law enforcement officials, health personnel, teachers, merchants, farm experts and others who live among but are not members of the local societies. Such agents deal directly with individuals of the local society in the absence of local organizations or associations which can perform appropriate functions.[6]

Implicit in Steward's comment is that when there is an effective organizational structure in the internally colonized territory the colonizer's task is simplified by working through that structure. In this light, the black elites are seen as a conduit through which the culture of the colonizers are channeled to the colonized masses. They become an effective mechanism of social control in the colonial process. In their roles as intermediaries, they are valuable to both the colonizers and the colonized masses. The black elite's role as intermediaries are discussed in greater

2

detail in other parts of this study. In this study Steward's category of mediating agents is synonymous with the category of colonizers.

In the colonial situation a degree of power is differentiated throughout the system, however, the ultimate power rests with the mother country. In the context of internal colonialism the ultimate power resides in the American society as a whole. The various components of the system, i.e., capitalist, colonizers, black bourgeoisie and the black masses are functionally related and their roles and authority are delineated within the system. Oppression and power in this system is relative to location within the system. There is a hierarchy of power with very little of it at the level of the oppressed masses to a great deal at the level of the colonizer.

Since power or the ability to effect decision making is relative to location in the structure it can be expected in the case of the lower classes that power is basically negative. The masses can and on occasion have withheld their services to the total system by the means of strikes, destruction of production tools and by boycotting the products of government and industry. An example of this type of power was demonstrated in the Memphis, New York and San Francisco garbage disposal strikes in recent times. Negative power of this sort sends shock waves throughout the entire system.

The black bourgeoisie's power must be viewed from at least three levels especially when their roles as intermediaries between the colonized masses and the colonizer are considered. Firstly, they must be seen as leaders for some segment of the colonized community by the colonizer or be considered as experts in fields useful to the colonizer to gain legitimacy. Secondly, the colonized masses should legitimize them as leaders and act toward the bourgeoisie in accordance with this definition. Thirdly, and perhaps most importantly, they must perceive themselves as being leaders.

The black elites who are recognized as leaders by the colonizers are granted discretionary power within their areas of competence. Hence, we find judges, attorneys, educators, heads of community programs and others likely situated with a certain amount of power within the system. Limits are placed on this power by the colonial authorities but their power tends to exceed that of the colonized masses. To the extent they are legitimized by the colonized masses, they have an additional power base. Coupled with the discretionary power received from the colonizer is the negative power of the colonized masses.

Their perceptions of themselves as leaders of intermediaries are crucial to any exercise of power. If they perceive themselves as powerless they cannot be expected to utilize power. A situation of this magnitude would necessarily lead to direct control of the colony by the colonizers. It would be incorrect to assume this group is entirely powerless because it does not own the means of production or have great political clout. It would be more accurate to conclude their power is limited by their position in the socio-economic and political structure.

The internal colonized elites have a significant role in relationship to the means of production. From their positions of prominence in the colonized community, they are able to mobilize the masses in the area of modernization. By conspicuous consumption and through educational and religious institutions, the colonized bourgeoisie plays a crucial role in modernizing the masses. They are the principal conduit of Western European culture to the colonized. Further, in general they are the articulators of the desires and aspirations of the masses to the dominant society. A great deal of the responsibility of modernizing the internally colonized rests with the intermediary class. It is through their roles as intermediaries the internal colonized bourgeoisie becomes identified with the means of production and to some extent with the elements of oppression in a capitalist society.

Too often the bourgeoisie's roles in relation to the means of production and the transmission of Western culture are emphasized and their immense contributions to the colonized as articulators of the concerns of the colonized for a better life are ignored. The characteristics of a colonized elite class often places it in a position that draws criticism from both the dominate power and the oppressed who they are trying to assist in finding a niche in Western society. When the colonized becomes destructive or disorderly the colonizers are apt to look critically at this class and doubt their effectiveness as leaders. On the other hand, they become a scape-goat group when the promises of the greater society are not fulfilled. They become objects of derision and criticism. They are accused by the oppressed of being the major tools in their oppression. The aloofness of this class, their secret organizations and in some cases their skin color are objects of suspicion and distrust. In spite of this seemingly unending abuse the colonized bourgeoisie must maintain some perspective of their roles. The masses will generally find it is in their interest to rely upon their leadership in securing a niche in the process of modernization.

Investigation clearly indicates, members of the internally colonized bourgeoisie in terms of the American experience has a clear perception of its leadership role. They have been in the forefront of much of the progress made by the colonized in a capitalist dominated society. Every generation has produced great leaders such as Frederick Douglass, Martin Delaney, Booker T. Washington, W. E. B. Dubois, Malcom X and Martin Luther King among the colonized. The Dynamics of the society are such that there has always been leaders who have led and inspired the colonized to a higher level of political, social and economic achievement. The weight of the historical evidence indicates leaders of the colonized were deeply committed to achieving better living conditions for the less fortunate. As a class they were not indifferent to the plight of the oppressed. It is easy to select a few of the great leaders from this class and to extol their virtues but more realistically this dedication to the masses was not limited to a few prominent men.

Many among the colonized bourgeoisie who will remain nameless in the pages of history, devoted their time and energies to religious and educational institutions, banks and insurance companies, clubs and fraternal organizations that established homes for the aged, orphaned children and provided services otherwise unobtainable by the colonized in the dominate community. There were those who waged individual battles against oppression and prejudice in labor unions, the courts and other institutions who will not receive credit for their unselfish and courageous sacrifices. As a class, the colonized bourgeoisie has contributed to the survival of the masses in many adverse situations.

There is danger in simply indicating the contributions of the black bourgeoisie. The danger is, one may over generalize to the point some of the shortcomings of this class are overlooked. The facts are that in addition to the contributions of the black bourgeoisie made to the progress of the American blacks, there were some who took advantage of their positions to further exploit the oppressed. Some utilized their relative affluence, associational ties and fraternal organizations to enhance class prestige. In some instances these ties contributed to an aloofness from lower classes of the colonized.

E. Franklin Frazier found that the black bourgeoisie lived ina world of make-believe and black society was a status without the material substances to support

4

their position. He indicated the activity of black society served to differentiate the black bourgeoisie from the masses of poorer blacks and at the same time compensate for the exclusion of the black bourgeoisie from the larger white community.

Historically, the roots of the bourgeoisie were among the house servants who enjoyed a certain prestige among the other slaves on the plantation during their social gatherings. This was the group most likely to be set free or educated by their masters. This class of servants were more likely to be of light skin color through their closer contacts with slave owners. By virtue of their relations with the family of slave owners, they became the conduit through which Western culture was filtered to the black masses. In some instances unwittingly, they became tools of the colonial system in eradicating Afro-American culture while exhorting the virtues of Western culture. There are indications this characterization of the black bourgeoisie is rapidly changing. It would be improper to ignore the contributions of this class and any discussion of them that eliminated the deleterious aspects of this class would be inadequate.[7]

For purposes of definition, this class must be viewed as it relates to the economic base of the black masses. In view of the class perceptions of the group and others who act toward them as a class, their economic base decreases in relevance. The occupational groupings of the bourgeoisie as seen by Frazier is as follows:

> Professional and technical personnel, principally school teachers, preachers, physicians, dentists, lawyers, college professors, entertainers, embalmers, funeral directors, social workers, and nurses and a sprinkling of persons in the technical occupations such as architecture, engineering and chemistry; 2) Managers, offials and proprietors (exclusion of farm owners) largely buyers, postmasters, public administration officials, credit men, purchasing agents, shippers of farm products, railroad conductors, union officials and proprietors of business enterprises; 3) Clerical and sales workers, including bank tellers, bookkeepers, cashiers, secretaries, stenographers, telephone and telegraph operators, mail carriers and railway mail clerks; 4) Craftsmen, foremen and kindred workers which constitutes on the whole the lower-middle class and is therefore identified with the black bourgeoisie.[8]

Frazier indicates the median income of Negro families in the United States in 1949 was $1,665 or fifty-one percent of the median income of white families which was $3,232. Sixteen percent of the white families had incomes of $3,000. For the Country as a whole, the incomes of the black or the black bourgeoisie range from between $2,000 and $2,500 and upwards. The majority of their incomes did not amount to as much as $4,000 and only one-half of one percent of them had an income of $5,000 or more. He maintains that these incomes show clearly that the black bourgeoisie is comprised essentially of white-collar workers. Those who had incomes between $4,000 and $5,000 were at the top of the pyramid of the black bourgeoisie.[9]

The modernization process has increased the number of white-collar workers in the black community and the black bourgeoisie have made some gains in terms of income. The percentage of black white-collar workers increased from twenty-three percent in 1967 to thirty percent in 1972. This increase in the black middle class parallels increases in educational attainment. About one-half million or eighteen percent of all blacks 18 to 24 years old were enrolled in college in 1972, about double the 1967 level. The drop-out rate for those 18 to 24 year old blacks declined between 1967 and 1972 from 22.8 percent to 17.5 percent. Approximately ninety percent of the black 16 and 17 year-olds were enrolled in school in 1972 compared to eighty-four percent in 1967. The proportion of 20 to 29 year olds who were high school graduates rose from fifty-four percent in 1967 to sixty-five percent in 1972. The proportion of those 25 to 34 years old with four years of college or more increased from five to eight percent during the same period.[10]

The United States Department of Commerce, Social and Economic Statistics Administration, Bureau of Census indicates, "Family incomes for Negro and other races ... have risen substantially over the twenty-year period, 1951 to 1971. The proportion of families of Negro and other races with incomes below $3,000 (in constant 1971 dollars) declined from 47 percent in 1951 to 19 percent in 1971. The proportion with incomes of $10,000 or more increased from 3 percent to 30 percent during this period."[11] All areas of the country experienced an increase in the occupational level of black Americans. Utilizing Fraziers economic criteria, it is found that the largest growth in the black bourgeoisie was in the West with seventy percent of the Negro and other population in the middle level and higher paid occupations: sixty-nine percent in the North and fifty percent in the South. In analyzing these statistics a great deal of caution is urged. The statistics, in regards to the West and North, obviously include high income racial groups that are now black, e.g., the Japanese Americans. The Southern statistics would include Blacks, Native Americans and Mexican Americans. Demographic realities dictates this caution. Demographic considerations notwithstanding, it seems reasonable to conclude there has been significant increases in the black bourgeoisie and these increases are sociologically and economically salient in terms of leadership and direction in the black community. · It should be pointed out that most of the increase in black income is related to expanded governmental bureaucracies and the employment of blacks in white industries. In 1969 black owned firms accounted for approximately one percent of total American Business sales and blacks owned less than three percent of the wealth of the country. The expanded economic base of the black middle-class has effect on the characteristics of the bourgeoisie: These effects are important in this study.[12]

The Study

In this study, this writer makes a selective study of the Oakland black elite who have historically fulfilled the role of intermediaries between the black masses and the white power structure. A better understanding of this elite is necessary in analyzing the behavior of the colonized minority, their responses to oppression and their efforts to improve the conditions of the colonized minority. The historic role of the middle class as intermediaries within the framework of the internal colonization model will be explored.

It is the intent of this study to determine how the Afro-American elites of Oakland define their position and those of black-Americans generally, in regards to the concepts of internal colonization and internal modernization. Further, this study will analyze their definitions of their situations as intermediaries, i.e., from their points of view whether they consider themselves as an elite; are they spokesmen for the black community in their fields of expertise? Do they feel they have a special obligation to the black community? Do they feel their primary obligations are to their employers, who are usually members of the dominant race and their perceptions of the most pressing problems confronting the colonized in the Oakland area. Other data analyzed in this study includes: attitude on school bussing and their attitudes on integration and black nationalism.

Much has been made of the fact black Americans, like many groups in American society are not a homogeneous group. It has been stated, especially by those who initiate oppressive actions that there are blacks of all political, social and economic persuasions from the far right to the far left. The validity of this assertion is unassailable but there is a danger of pressing these generalizations too far. Black Americans are no more or less capable of gathering, sorting and analyzing all of the information relative to them than any other group in a complex modernizing world. To offset their individual lack of expertise in certain areas they must rely on opinion makers and other leaders to fulfill this function. In this connection, the perceptions of the leadership class are crucial in terms of race relations and public policy.

Site of Study

Oakland, California has been chosen as the site of this study. The city is particularly suitable for this study because it is considered by many to be an all-American city. In many ways this characterization of the City of Oakland is valid. Oakland has all of the major problems associated with urbanization, i.e., a large minority population, inadequate housing, flight to the suburbs by the white population and industry, dwindling tax base, increased demands for city services and increasing militancy on the part of the poor and deprived.

Although this is not an economic study, it should be pointed out that Oakland has a market-directed economy. The vast majority of the economic institutions are privately owned. Basically, Oakland is an example of urban American capitalism, but much of this is being changed by the necessity of providing services to those who are unable to pay for them. There is a growing competition between the Federal government, local economic institutions, politicians and the organized poor to control the economic and politics of the area. It is this competition that has brought about this new urban elite that is one of the concerns of this paper.

Oakland has a reformed city government. The government consists of a strong city manager, a relatively weak mayor and a city council. This ensures that the power elite of local politics can maintain control of the allocation of the resources available to the community. Oakland public officials are required to run for office on non-partisan ballots. The effect of this is that political control has been kept in the hands of a Republican minority in Oakland often frustrating the efforts of the Democrats and ethnic minorities in their quest for change. It also effectively perpetuates the business tie with the political institutions that operate the city in many instances to the noticeable disadvantage of the poor.[13]

The problems that promoted the development of the new elite in the 1960's are similar to those in many cities. The poorest part of the city is adjacent to the central business district. In this area in 1966-67 the sub-employment rate was 30 percent. The racial composition of this area consists of 60 percent black and 8 percent Mexican American. The total unemployed, not looking for work, and subemployed in the flatlands was 47 percent of the total work force of this area for the same period of time. In 1960, 39.6 percent of all whites in Oakland were living in deprivation or poverty; 66.1 percent of all non-whites were in deprivation-or-worse categories.[14]

The income and unemployment situations in the city of Oakland has not changed significantly in the past decade. However, overt acts of militancy such as riots and destruction of private property has decreased from the violence-prone sixties.

In the city of Oakland in 1971 the following income distribution for households was reported in the Sales Management Magazine; $3,000 and under income category 17.2 percent; 10.1 percent in the $3,000-$5,000 category; 18.9 percent in the $5,000-$8,000 category. It can be noted that Oakland has a population with approximately fifty percent of the area's households earning under the $9,328 average for the County of Alameda. By elementary reasoning it can be concluded that the situation in the flatlands exceeds by far these computations for the entire city.[15]

The foregoing compounded by racial discrimination of the housing industry in the suburbs surrounding Oakland has produced a ghetto-like atmosphere in the core city. The immediate consequences of this shortage in housing has led to a high rent structure for the city generally, especially where the poor and non-whites are located. In Oakland as well as other cities the evidence indicates the poor pay a larger percentage of their income for housing than the more affluent. In 1968 the average rents in Oakland for a one bedroom apartment ran between $90 and $125; yet the rent paying ability of Oakland's poverty-class population in that year was between $40 and $80 per month. In the San Francisco-Oakland area, 25.1 percent of the non-white families pay in excess of one third of their income for rent. It is not uncommon in West Oakland for home owners to have a third mortgage at flagrantly exorbitant rates of interest, conditions which in themselves account in a large measure for keeping the poor in poverty.[16]

The housing situation in the city is aggravated by the wide scale destruction of large amounts of existing low-rent units that are seldom replaced by any governmental agency. This destruction places an additional strain on the poverty areas because they absorb most of those tenants who cannot afford the more expensive rentals in the suburbs.

The city of Oakland was selected for this study because it has one of the largest and oldest concentrations of black-Americans in Northern California. It has a tradition of leadership of the black East Bay communities. Indeed, the first East Bay black church, The First African Methodist Episcopal Church, followed by Beth Eden Baptist Church, was founded in the city near the turn of the century. The First African Methodist Episcopal Church established the first school for black children in Oakland. Prior to this time, black children attended schools on white campuses in segregated classrooms. Many of the traditional elites mentioned in this study can trace their legitimacy from these institutions as well as from secret organizations and through black entrepreneurship. The migration of black-Americans to the Oakland area during and after World War II placed an enormous strain on these institutions that were in some instances designed to mitigate oppression and promote modernization.

In Oakland in 1967, over 140 Federal programs were spending at an annual rate of almost one hundred million dollars. About twenty-four million was channeled specifically into poverty and job training programs. Hayes reports the breakdown of this money as follows:

Big business (four corporations)	$ 6,880,000
Government (five local and county agencies)	10,950,000
Alameda County Central Labor Council	1,500,000
Minority groups (three groups)	158,000
Negro ministers (one group)	60,000
Small business (two groups)	185,000
Mixed (business, labor, minorities)	4,600,000
Total	$25,333,000[17]

8

The new elite who were elevated to administer these federal programs were augmented on the state and local level by others who were called upon to attack the social and economic problems of the residents of Oakland. In many cases this elite attempted to maintain their credibility with the masses by avoiding conspicuous associational ties with the traditional elites who were in some instances considered too conservative to bring about meaningful social change.

Frazier's detailed definition of the black middle class has proved to be useful. Income in excess of $8,000 per year, occupation and social status as indicated by associational ties were the criteria utilized in designating the black middle class for the purposes of this study.[18] In this study the black middle class has been divided into two analytical groups, traditional and new urban elites. From an understanding of these groups it is felt that a meaningful understanding of the sociological implications of political and economic actions in the black community will be facilitated.

The East Bay Area Club of the National Association of Negro Business and Professional Women's Clubs, Inc., the Oakland Chamber of Commerce, the Coro Foundation, the Community Action Program, the Oakland City Managers Office, the Manpower Development Program, the West Oakland Planning Commission, the Model Cities Program, the Oakland Redevelopment Agency, the New Careers Program, the Neighborhood Youth Program, the Concentrated Employment Program, the Oakland Economic Development Corporation, Incorporated and the West Oakland Health Center were utilized in compiling data for the selection of a population for sampling.

The interviews on which this study is based were conducted in the Spring and Summer of 1973, at a time when overt civil rights activity appeared to be declining and racial-militant student and racial confrontations were no longer a daily phenomenon in American life. Blacks were to a degree integrated into the administrative apparatus of the Oakland City government, the Superintendents office of the Board of Education, the poverty programs and the Board of Commissioners of the Port of Oakland.

A list of seven hundred middle-class blacks was compiled through preliminary research and with the cooperation of the organizations previously mentioned. Three hundred and fifty new urban elites and three hundred and fifty traditional elites were selected for the population in order of their appearance on the lists presented to the researcher.[19] In view of the growth of the black middle-class since 1950, it was necessary to rely on organizations with previous research in the field for the names, addresses and in some instances, associational ties of the population. The East Bay Area Club of the National Association of Negro Business and Professional Women's Clubs, Inc., and the Coro Foundation made available to the researcher their lists of black business owners, professionals, fraternities and other elites both traditional and new urban. These lists were supplemented by rosters from the agencies mentioned above to accumulate the best information available to the researcher on blacks in the elite category.

Ten percent of the blacks listed were systematically selected for interviews. The elites who were employed in organizations in the public sector that are a direct outgrowth of the Civil Rights Movement in the 1960's and those who were employed by the federal government were classified as the new urban elite population. All others were considered traditional elites. The two elite groups were placed in separate rotating files and each tenth name was selected for interview. If the name card indicated a black business or organization, the owner or designated organization representative was interviewed.

In all, seventy interviews were conducted with blacks who met the criteria as middle-class, bourgeoisie or elites. These terms, for the purposes of this study are used interchangeably. Thirty-five of the interv iews were conducted with the traditional elites. A more detailed description of these elites is dis- cussed in the following chapters. Legitimacy for the new urban elites usually is institutionalized in governmental structures, bureaucracies and in private or- ganizations that emerged largely in the black community to aid and facilitate the allocation of resources produced as a result of the many and diverse programs that followed the social unrest of the 1960's.

The explicit dichotomy immediately foregoing notwithstanding, there is a degree of ambiguity in dividing black elites into two groups. As an example, elected politicians, teachers and professors have legitimacy in both the black community and with outside structures. They may have high status and class in both the black community and the dominant community simultaneously. For the purposes of this study this problem has been resolved as follows: elected offi- cials who achieved their positions through traditional methods and structures, i.e., through the established political processes are considered to be tradi- tional elites. This criteria is also useful in the case of educators or others. However, this does not pertain in instances where their positions are the result of direct funding for specific modernization projects of the government or similar agencies such as the East Bay Skills Center, established under the Manpower De- velopment Training Act of 1964. The administrators, teachers and others in the latter group are defined as part of the new black elites.

It should be noted that the problem persists when associational or fraternal ties are considered solely as defining criteria. In some instances, members of both elite groups may be members of and actively support the same traditional or conservative organizations in the black community, although available data indi- cates that the new urban elite are less likely to belong to one of these organiza- tions than the traditional black elite. There is some overlap. It is clear that these organizations somewhat reflect the divisions in the broader community, i.e., some of their members are more attuned to rising expectations of the black com- munity in general than they are with the conservative aspects of these particular organizations. Therefore, other criteria was necessary to define the new elites without excluding the variable of associational ties. For the purpose of this study the definition was broadened to include occupation, income and status in addition to associational ties for classification.

Additionally, status inconsistency appears to be generalized throughout the black community in the Oakland area. Traditional definitions of class and status have little relevancy to the empirical positions of persons in the community. Therefore, class variables such as income, education, occupation, residence and association may be only tangentially related to high status. Status is defined here as all persons who are accorded the same estimations of social honor or pres- tige. In the community it is not uncommon to find that a minister who is prominent politically and held in high esteem by the community at large may have a low income and is a member of a low prestige church or a member of the West Oakland Planning Commission. His income, residence and education may not be congruent with his position in the community.[20]

In speaking of the dichotomy in the black middle class, Charles V. Hamilton suggests:

"The black middle-class that began to develop after the Civil War and on into the turn of the century tended to be largely a private sector black middle-class , artisans mostly. They derived their income from the private sector, and, as we know, many of them had a large or, in some instances, exclusive white clientele. Some black barbers in the South only cut white men's hair. Some black caterers catered only for whites. Such a group could develop class interest antagonistic to the black lower classes. I am suggesting this is not true today."[21]

Black Americans in the Greater Oakland Area

Participants in recent urban unrest have included Afro-Americans from various levels of the socio-economic hierarchy. To the extent black leadership roles are exercised by the bourgeoisie, their perceptions of problems confronting Afro-Americans are sociologically relevant. Much of the violent reaction to racial oppression in the 1960's was centered in the general area of Oakland, California. Therefore, the Oakland black bourgeoisie's perception of accomplishments in the preceding three decades and their attitudes toward change becomes increasingly important. Further, it is important to assess E. Franklin Frazier's conception of the black bourgeoisie in the light of educational and economic changes since 1950. As previously indicated, the economic base of the black bourgeoisie has expanded and Frazier's contention that "as a consequence of their isolation, the majority of the black bourgeoisie live in a cultural vacuum and their lives are devoted largely to fatuities"[22] may no longer be valid in this Western city.

Since all institutions political, social and economic do not modernize at the same rate of speed, this study will indicate the areas the black community will focus on in seeking their goal of equal opportunity and full partnership in the American society in the 1970's. This study will consist of a socio-historical analysis of the black American's position in American society. The historical analysis of national trends in the modernization of black Americans places in proper perspective the concerns of the Oakland black bourgeoisie. Problems of adaptation, such as racial integration, separation, political and economic integration have both historical and nation-wide ramifications. The local actions of the colonized cannot be understood outside of the context of an overview of the entire picture of the dynamics in the process of modernizing a previously enslaved people. Actions of the black Americans in other regions of the country have effect on the Afro-Americans of Oakland, California. Conversely, actions of the Afro-Americans of Oakland, often have effect on the lives and aspirations of blacks in other regions of the Country.

In 1969, there were one hundred sixty-three thousand blacks owned businesses over two times as many as in 1930. They employed 151,996 people and had total receipts of four billion, five hundred thousand dollars.[23] Lerone Bennett, Jr. indicates that in 1969:

"The ten most important industries for black-owned firms were 1) automobile dealers and gasoline filling stations, 2) food stores, 3) wholesale trade, 4) eating and drinking places, 5) personal services, 6) special sales contractors, 7) miscellaneous retail stores, 8) general building contractors, 9) trucking and warehousing, 10) insurance carriers. The ten states with the largest number of black owned firms were California (14,689), Texas (12,740), Illinois (10,265), New York (9,269), Ohio (9,193), Pennsylvania (7,687), Virginia (7,229) and Georiga (6,708). Some 34 percent of the black

11

owned firms with 34 percent of the total receipts were concentrated in California, Texas, Illinois, New York and Ohio.[24]

One of the concerns of this study is to determine to what extent, if any, the differences in economic base of the traditional elites who generally have an economic and political base in the black community and the new urban elites whose economic base is predominately in governmental organizations and white industry are reflected in their attitudes toward problems pertaining to black Americans. It is also a legitimate concern of this study to ascertain whether there are differences of opinion as to the method of achieving equality for blacks when the source of income is considered i.e., if the source of income is important in terms of whether an individual prefers racial separation or integration.

Black Americans arrived in California with the Spanish settlers in the Seventeenth Century.[25] Their migration to the States have generally followed the pattern of white migration. The black population of California increased significantly during the period of the great gold rush of 1849, but available evidence indicates they did not reach Alameda County (Oakland is a part of Alameda County) in great numbers until during and after the period of National Reconstruction. The black population of Alameda County was five thousand persons in 1915. They brought with them skills that were in short supply in the west. They established businesses, fraternal and social organizations, churches, schools and organizations to care for orphaned children and the aged. Along with other groups they played a vital part in building the West.[26]

The early black pioneers to the Oakland area, were deeply concerned with the plight of their race and they were dedicated to improving the lot of black Americans. Some of them were professional people who saw an opportunity for Afro-Americans to gain a measure of success not offered in other parts of the country. They had a commitment to other blacks especially in the South, who were suffering the severe hardships of racism and discrimination. The black middle-class founded newspapers that were to keep blacks informed of matters of interest and to the extent the black media was controlled by the bourgeoisie, they became a conduit on acceptable standards of behavior. This control of the press placed the bouregoisie in the position of being the class most instrumental in modernizing black communities and in socializing them to urban living. The concern of the bourgeoisie with the plight of black Americans across the nation creates a very difficult situation when an attempt is made to analyze the actions of blacks in any specific region of the country because their perceptions of the racial situation nationally has effect on their local actions.

The following two articles in black newspapers near the turn of the century are indicative of both the interest of the black bourgeoisie in other in different areas of the country and their role in mobilizing the black community for improvement:

"The lynching record of 1907 will show a decided improvement over that of 1906, the total for the current year to date being forty-two--three Negro women, four white men and thirty-five Negro men. The record includes only cases of unmistakable lynchings, leaving out those in which victims were killed by pursuing posses while resisting capture. The record for the last year was seventy-two being thirty more than that of 1907.[27]

OPPORTUNITIES FOR THE NEGRO IN OAKLAND AND SAN FRANCISCO

There is a tide in the affairs of men, which taken at its flood, leads on to happiness; omitted, all the balance of their lives is bounded in shadows and misery

12

Now is the "flood tide" in the affairs of the Negro of Oakland and San Francisco ...

The question is will he grasp it or let it pass by?

Land bought twenty or thirty years ago for a song has been sold during the past year for a fortune, but there is the same opportunity to buy land how which in a similar period of time can be sold to equal advantage ...

Help is needed in most branches of government service, and the civil service examinations are open to all who wish to take them.

A number of clerical positions and other positions of trust are held by our young men and some opportunity is open for others.

Of domestic servants, the demand always exceeds the supply.

A large number of new buildings being erected require laborers.[28]

The black press in the Oakland area, in addition to the above, counselled black residents on their behavior, clothing and proper attitudes. It strongly supported church attendance and Christian endeavors. It provided a method of introducing new black arrivals of prominence to the community. The black press attempted to raise political consciousness and organization and in 1909 the Oakland Sunshine was advocating community control. "What the Sunshine would like to see, a colony of our people in every county in the State with the community under Negro rule."[29] The black press played an important part in recruiting black migrants to California in the early part of the century.

Community control was a slogan and was never achieved in the Oakland Area. However, the newspapers were successful in persuading blacks to migrate to the West. A summary of the black community of the East Bay in 1929 is as follows:

"Colored population of 18,000 inhabitants, 25 churches, 33 lodges, 27 art, business and social clubs, 8 tailoring establishments, 2 undertaking companies, 1 pharmacy, 1 wholesale and retail ice cream dealer, 2 grocers, 16 barber shops, 5 printers, 2 homes for the aged, 1 children's home and day nursery, 2 insurance companies, 2 haberdasheries, 4 confectionary and sweetshops, 15 restaurants and cafes, 3 garages, 11 billiard and pool parlors, 13 beauty parlos, 2 art and mechanical studios, 2 adjustment organizations, 2 jewelers, 1 business league, 8 modistes and dressmakers, 1 medical and dental association, 9 physicians, 4 dentists, 16 real estate brokers, 1 YMCA and 1 YWCA, 2 finance companies, 5 furniture stores."[30]

The black bourgeoisie in Oakland was dynamic and displayed a great deal of expertise in the professions, businesses and organizations. In many ways they were an important element in developing a viable sense of community among local Afro-Americans. On the other hand, some tended to isolate themselves socially and economically from the masses of blacks. An article appearing in the Oakland Independent in 1910 criticizes a local sorority for snobery during the annual turn out sermon at a local church. They were cautioned that their attitudes were not in the best interest of the community. "In many instances it results in a complete loss to the weaker students, of the purpose of a college course. Be careful lest you make snobs, these which there is no more useless being on this earth, and particularly in our race at its present stage of development."[31]

Although it is considered judicious in some circles to overlook the importance of skin color in the internal stratification of Afro-American society, the evidence

13

is overwhelming that the degree of darkness of skin was important in social and economic life. The importance of skin color in the local community of Oakland will be addressed in this study. Skin color was extremely important among the early black bourgeoisie as indicated in the following quotes from the Oakland Sunshine in 1915:

> "... now it is a well-known fact that out here in the west we have many of that kind who are no good to the race. They are shunning Negro company; but for the loaves and fishes they hang on to some Negro societies and are wont to be seen and heard in large gatherings. The Sunshine denounces this kind of Negro. They are a menace to race progress."[32]

> "We would like to ask a few of our big race men to practice a little oftener what they preach and help the race along lines other than hot air and pondering to those Negroes that are passing, as they call it. Just please stay on one side and don't keep flopping back and forth. We Simon Pures don't need you. Keep passing."[33]

The secrecy associated with the middle-class fraternal organizations and the interaction between fraternal organizations, social clubs, The Negro Business League and traditional advocacy organizations such as the National Association for the Advancement of Colored People supported the class division among members of the Afro-American community. Logic dictates the isolation and snobbery of some of the black middle-class had effect on their ability or willingness, upon occasion, to respond to the needs of the black lower classes. This black middle-class developed a class consciousness in social and economic areas that widened the cleavage between the classes as indicated below. This class division in conjunction with the secrecy of the fraternal organizations tended to foster suspicion among the lower classes. The Oakland Sunshine published an editorial in 1915 on the proper conduct of members of fraternal organizations that clearly indicates the nature of these associations. The editorial states in part:

> "Under the above heading we made reference last week to the Samaritan part played by a minister in one of our small towns. We now bring the lesson nearer home and apply it to our fraternal societies. It is frequently said lodges do not practice their preaching outside their lodge rooms and that brothers in the same lodges frequently overlook each other when they have matters of business to transact and patronage to disburse. It is claimed that they will spend their money just as willingly with a non-brother as with one of the craft. Now if this is true it is a grievous error and out of harmony with their social obligation. Lodge members should be bound together by a sympathetic tie and that tie should be love and concern for each other's welfare, a keeper of my brother's affairs ... Some societies are more binding than others and are more efficient ... Brothers in societies should appreciate their fellow-members in business and give them preference in all business matters. If running a show, a meat, crockery or hardware store, they should be found constantly at his car and around his place of business.[34]

Current Demographic Considerations

The number of urbanized areas with twenty percent or more of the population black has only increased from four in 1950 to five today. However, the number of central cities with twenty percent of the population black has increased from six in 1950 to twenty-three in 1970; while the number of suburban rings surrounding these cities centers that have ten to twenty percent of their populations black has decreased from five in 1950 to two in 1970.[35]

The current population of Oakland is 361,561. Thirty-five percent of the population is black and twenty-siven percent of the black population are home owners. In 1970 the mean household income was $7,793 for blacks and other races. Their income represents 7.7 percent of the aggregate income for the residents of Oakland. This income percentage does not compare favorably with their percentage of the total population.[36]

The city of Oakland has two major geographic areas that have sociological and econoomical implications. There is a large area known as the flatlands. The flatlands consists of the City Center and the homes of those who tend to be in the lower socio-economic category. It is generally populated by new migrants of all races, blacks, Chicanos and Chinese Americans. This area is surrounded by the hill area of Oakland, Berkeley and Piedmont on one side and the Oakland waterfront on the other side. The hill area is comparatively affluent in that property values and incomes tend to be higher than the flatlands and there are few pockets of poverty in them.

The 1970 census reveals in the flatland areas where there is a concentration of Afro-Americans, there are 7,279 black white--collar workers, 1,462 professional and technical persons, 743 in the area of management and administration, 556 blacks in sales, 4,418 in clerical positions and 9,950 blacks who are blue collar workers. This large segment of the black bourgeoisie with its potential for leadership as outlined above, who resides in the relatively poverty stricken areas of the city is of increasing importance in analyzing the directions Afro-Americans will focus upon in their quest for equality in Oakland, California. Many of the black bourgeoisie live in close proximity to the lower classes. It can be expected in view of this close contact significant numbers of the bourgeoisie will identify with the aspirations of the lower class. Although it would be utopian to expect all traces of exclusion to vanish, many of the artificial barriers between the classes should disappear in view of the constant interaction between members of both classes. If the black middle-class exerts its traditional leadership of the lower classes it then can be expected that agitation from the blacks as a whole will be directed toward economic advancement, improved housing, education and other material gains associated with middle-class values. If their leadership is effective, an analysis of the bourgeoisie should reveal the areas in which social change is likely to occur in the black community within the next decade.

It is the purpose of this study to analyze the attitudes of the black bourgeoisie of Oakland, California in regards to their perceptions and priorities for change in the black community. The internal colonialist model of race relations will be discussed in Chapter 2. The theories of E. Franklin Frazier, Albert Memmi, Robert Blauner, Jean Sartre, Franz Fanen and others will be examined. The roles of the black bourgeoisie in terms of this model will be discussed.

In Chapter 3, the internal modernization process will be investigated. Internal modernization involves the process whereby an economically, politically and culturally deprived people within the geographic area of a modern state, modernizes and acquires technological, political, social and economic modernization and fits into the niche of an existing modern system on a basis of equality. Essential to internal modernization is the reality many of the decisions crucial to the process are made by a dominate group who have the ultimate power.

The role of the black bourgeoisie will be analyzed in relation to the modernization process. The black bourgeoisie has been divided into two groups, the traditional black bourgeoisie (members of sororities, fraternities, secret associations and clubs, traditional protest groups such as the National Association for the Advancement of Colored People and the National Urban League) and the new urban elite who tend to have their source of legitimacy in the dominate power structure. Many of the new elite or black bourgeoisie receive their incomes from the public sector. A more detailed description of these elites can be found in Chapter 3.

REFERENCES TO CHAPTER 1

1. Feuer, Lewis S., ed. <u>Marx and Engles</u> (Garden City: Doubleday and Company, Inc., 1959) p. 15.

2. David E. Apter, <u>Chana in Transition</u> (New York: Anthepeum Press, 1968) p. 82.

3. Ibid., p. 125.

4. Frantz Fanon, <u>The Wretched of the Earth</u> (New York: Grove Press, Inc., 1968) p. 7.

5. Albert Memmi, <u>The Colonizer and the Colonized</u> (Boston: Beacon Press, 1965) pp. 1-76.

6. Julian H. Steward, ed., <u>Three African Tribes in Transition</u> (Chicago: University of Illinois Press, 1967) p. 14.

7. E. Franklin Frazier, <u>Black Bourgeoisie</u> (London: Collier-Macmillan, 1957) p. 162.

8. Lerone Bennett, Jr., <u>Black Bourgeoisie Revisited</u>, Ebony Vol. XXVIII, No. 10, August 1973, p. 52.

9. Frazier, op. cit., pp. 45-49.

10. U.S. Dept. of Commerce, <u>The Social and Economic Status of the Black Population</u>, Current Reports, July 1973, p. 3.

11. Ibid., p. 19.

12. Ibid.

13. Edward C. Hayes, <u>Power Structure and Urban Policy: Who Rules in Oakland?</u> (New York: McGraw-Hill Book Co., 1972) pp. 27-36.

14. Ibid., p. 46.

15. The Oakland Tribune, August 17, 1972, p. 7.

16. Hayes, op. cit., p. 67.

17. Ibid.

18. Occupations include professional and technical personnel, managers officials and proprieters; clerical and sales workers, i.e., bank tellers, bookkeepers, etc.; and craftsmen and foremen. Members of fraternities, sororities, the Black Elks (BPOE), Odd Fellows, the Masons were considered to have middle class status for the purpose of this study.

19. All of the respondents selected for this study re-ponded to the interviews. The actual interviews lasted from one and a half hours to four hours.

20. St. Clair Drake and Horace R. Cayton, "Black Metropolis" (New York: Harcourt, Brace and World, Inc., 1962) pp. 661-662.

21. Alex Peinsett, Class Patterns in Black Politics, Ebony, Vol. XXVIII, No. 10, August 1973, p. 35.

22. Frazier, op. cit., p. 46.

23. Lerone Bennett, Jr., The Quest for Economic Security, Ebony, February 1974, pp. 77-79.

24. Ibid.

25. Carey McWilliams, North from Mexico (New York: Greenwood Press, Publishers, 1968) p. 36.

26. The Oakland Sunshine, October 15, 1907.

27. The Oakland Sunshine, December 21, 1907, p. 1.

28. Ibid.

29. The Oakland Sunshine, September 11, 1909, p. 3.

30. The Oakland Independent, December 19, 1929, p. 2.

31. The Oakland Independent, May 30, 1910, p. 1.

32. The Oakland Sunshine, August 7, 1915, p. 4.

33. The Oakland Sunshine, August 18, 1915, p. 1.

34. The Oakland Sunshine, July 24, 1915, p. 1.

35. Albert I. Hermalin and Reynold Farley, Potential for Residential Integration in Cities and Suburbs: Implications for Busing Controversy, American Sociological Review, July 1973, p. 600.

36. United States Department of Commerce, Bureau of Census Consumer Income, July 1973, p. 2.

Chapter 2

AFRO-AMERICAN RESPONSES TO INTERNAL COLONIZATION

In Oakland the black bourgeoisie reflects the historical division within the class. The black elites seldom agree to the course of action the black community should take to gain equality and justice. These attitudes and responses, deeply rooted in Afro-American history, are between integrationists and separatists approaches and between cultural and economic-political emphasis. Each response has its proponents and leaders among the black bourgeoisie and the battle ground for leadership is the black masses who tend to respond differentially to the various segments of the bourgeoisie. In many cases these responses appear to be utilitarian in that the masses seemingly respond to the particular viewpoint, given time and place, that is most likely to produce positive results.

The Oakland black bourgeoisie is a product of these historical forces within the black community. As indicated in the preceding chapter, the black middle class has provided leadership in terms of political, social and economic action since the first blacks arrived in the Oakland area in significant numbers. Afro-Americans have always had black leaders and organizations with varying degrees of militance espousing the different viewpoints on black responses to white oppression. It is important to understand the actions of the local black bourgeoisie of Oakland do not take place in isolation. Indeed, historical and nationwide imperatives often alter the perceptions of the black bourgeoisie with respect to the feasibility of programs and actions. To the extent these imperatives are perceived and acted upon by the bourgeoisie, they are significant to this study of the black bourgeoisie. It is essential that one has a notion of the historical dynamics relating to the Black bourgeoisie if this is to be correctly interpreted in the light of evolving Afro-American thought and action. The respondents were asked to indicate which way black Americans are going at this time and which way they would prefer them to go. The results:

Table 1

WHICH WAY BLACK AMERICA

Reply to: "Which way black-Americans was the title of a recent Ebony issue. Which of the following comes closest to where you believe black people are going?"

	Traditional Elites (percent)	New Urban Elites (percent)
Integration	14	57
Political autonomy	46	17
Cultural autonomy	29	23
Assimilation	9	9
Separation	11	5

*More than 100%. More than one response.

Table 2

PREFERENCE OF DIRECTION

Reply to: "Now, for yourself, which way do you personally prefer black Americans to go?"

	Traditional Elites (percent)	New Urban Elites (percent)
Integration	17	37
Political autonomy	11	17
Cultural autonomy	26	29
Assimilation	14	9
Separation	6	3
No response	26	0
Total	100	100

To some extent all of the responses of Afro-Americans to oppression in America has failed to bring equality to American blacks. A more accurate picture would indicate there has been gradual progress toward equality in several areas. The reality of the present situation is, in spite of limited success in certain areas the black Americans in Oakland are far from their goal and the progress that has been achieved has been through a combination of approaches to the problems involved. At this time, as this study will indicate, there is considerable ambiguity as to the appropriate response of Afro-Americans.

The Position of Afro-Americans

Through the history of the black man in America, periodically groups and black leaders have publically rejected this country as their homeland and formed movements to migrate to other areas. As an oppressed people they have contended that in the United States their status is one of a colonized people in a society dominated by a white majority. In the perspective of these groups, the sole reason that the community seeks to preserve the black presence in America is that blacks are a necessary human resource and are exploited for the economic, political, psychological and social benefit of the dominant race. An abundance of evidence is submitted in support of this contention along with an examination of the circumstances surrounding the black man's appearance in this hemisphere which lends credence to this point of view.

The data indicates that many in the middle class feel that there is some movement in this country toward some form of integration and assimilation. Further, a plurality of the respondents indicates this is the proper course for the Afro-Americans to take. However, a substantial number of both black elite groups do not feel this is the proper direction for black aspirations and they reject this solution to the racial problems in America in favor of political or cultural autonomy. This is profoundly significant when most of the sociological literature and many social scientists have held that America is a melting pot and minorities should be integrated or assimilated in the manner of European immigrants. The possibilities of conflict between the races is heightened by these differences in perceptions of the white society and the black community. There is also the possibility of an intra-class struggle as proponents of different points of view in the middle class move to positions of leadership.

Clearly there is some concern in the black middle-class community of Oakland for integration but there is also an interest in gaining some power through political and cultural autonomy. The data do not indicate any general concensus in this class as to the direction of the class should lead the black masses and it can be pointed out that among the alternatives listed integration and assimilation has the most support. It is felt that this lack of cohesion makes this group highly manipulative by sell-organized smaller groups who can gain the support of parts of this middle-class in any given action and by the dominant power system that can play one segment of the middle class against the other for its own purposes, thereby, depriving the masses of the leadership that is necessary to resist oppression.

Table 3

INTERNAL COLONIZATION

Reply to: "Some scholars describe the blacks position in America as a colonized one. What is your reaction to this comment?"

	Traditional Elites (percent)	New Urban Elites (percent)
Blacks are colonized	31	31
Blacks are not colonized	23	26
No response	46	43
Total	100	100

In the black middle class of Oakland there is considerable support for the internal colonial theory, i.e., black people are a colonized group without significant power in American society. If members of the black middle-class perceive their situation as being colonized, it can be expected they will act in terms of this perception. The consequences of this definition of their situation may seriously impair the interaction between blacks and the majority racial group.

Organizations oriented toward separation of the races are prevalent among black Americans and they stretch across the entire political spectrum from far left to far right. Although these groups may not represent a majority of black opinion, their numbers are not insignificant and they are sociologically relevant to the study of American society as a whole. Some of them are Pan African oriented, that is, they identify directly with Africa, which is considered the motherland. Others emphasize separation within the confines of the United States. The essential point, however, is that they all have a common one basic premise, i.e., the black man's position in this country is not as an equal participant in the on-going process of American society and that he will never achieve equality. Further, some believe the white society is corrupt and it is no longer desirable or beneficial to the black race to join in this policies.

21

Students of American society and the black experience are utilizing the internal colonialist model in their analysis of this situation. By defining the blacks position as a colonial situation, the colonization process becomes a heuristic device by which we can explore the actions of both the dominant and subordinate populations and draw some conclusions as to the relevance of economic and social interactions of these groups. For instance, some of the immediate questions that evolve are what is the nature and method of domination over the black community? Is this domination comparable to traditional colonialism? Is there a black elite which is an intermediary between the two communities? What are the characteristics and predispositions of this elite? How do they affect social action?

The internal colonialist concept is particularly relevant to sociological investigation because it is a valid concept if it is perceived as such by significant numbers of affected people. Perception is an essential part of the human act. Therefore, if in ordering their world individuals or groups perceive their environment as constituting a colonial situation, their acts will be based upon this assumption. The study of the effects of the internal colonial process could conceivably involve a reinvestigation of such major areas of the social sciences as race relations, delinquent and deviant behavior and stratification.

Franz Fanon, speaking of this concept, describes the colonialized world as follows:

"The colonial world is a world cut in two. In capitalist societies the educational system whether lay or clerical the structure of moral reflexes handed down from father to son, the exemplary honesty of workers who are given a medal after fifty years of good and loyal service, and the affection which springs from harmonious relations and good behavior-- all these aesthetic expressions of respect for the established order serve to create around the exploited person an atmosphere of submission and of inhibition which lightens the task of policing considerably ..."

"This world divided into compartments, this world cut in two is inhibited by two different species. The originality of the colonial context is that economic reality, inequality, and the immense difference of ways of life never come to mask the human realities. When you examine at close quarters the colonial context, it is evident that what parcels out the world is to begin with the fact of belonging to a given race, a given species."[1]

In expounding upon the concept, Fanon emphasizes that when considering the colonial problem, the Marxist analysis should be stretched. Indeed, Marx saw the problems of Afro-Americans essentially as a lever to prod the proletarian revolution, overthrowing the bouregoisie and establishing proletarian rule. Marxist analysis does not take into account the variable of racism that is inherent in the colonial situation. Fanon indicates that "In colonies the economic structure is also a superstructure. The cause is the consequence; you are rich because you are white, you are white because you are rich."[2] This is equally true in the internal colonial situation.

One adherent to this theory, who has followed Fanon's lead is Stokely Carmichael, a black scholar and leader, who is now in self-imposed exile. Carmichael espouses a Pan-African ideology that holds "America does not belong to the blacks ... We are not black Americans. We are Africans."[3] It is his contention that other like-minded Americans with African ancestry should abandon the United States in a mass exodus. Certainly, as previously indicated most of these theories are not new.

In the internal colonialist model, especially in the American experience, the term colonizer refers to those of the majority race who control the institutions and apparatus of oppression. It includes those who actively or passively support individuals in the decision-making process who through their actions perpetuate the systematic denegration and exploitation of a people for the benefit of the dominant race. The exploitation has a psychological, economic, political and social dimension. In this situation all members of the dominant race tend to gain from the subordination of the exploited race, either directly or indirectly. This explanation of the concept colonizer should not be construed to include all of the members of the dominant race and it should not include those of the dominant race who have fought or resisted the forces of colonialization. There are many among the colonizer's race who have felt that colonial domination was unjust and inappropriate in American society. Some of these people have lost their lives in the struggle to relieve or mitigate oppression and others have been socially and politically ostracized for their actions and beliefs. When the term colonizer is utilized in this study, it does not include those in the category immediately foregoing.

The term colonized people refers to those who are systematically denied human, political, social and economic rights that are inherent in American citizenship. It refers to those who are exploited and held in a subordinate status either through the formal recognition of differences by the dominant power or through informal arrangements by those in the dominant race who are in positions to make decisions that affect the subordinate group. Realistically, if the subordination and exploitation of a people can be maintained without official or formal action of the government of the colonizer, there is little utility in taking formal or official notice of the oppression.

This study is based upon the premise that American society is colonial and the position of minority groups of color in this society are that of colonized peoples. It is clear that this premise, if accepted, explains some of the consequences of the socio-political and socio-economic systems. Further, the interactions of the two major components of a colonial situation, the colonizer and the colonized, can be analyzed in terms of this concept.

Early American Attitudes Toward Internal Colonization and Assimilation

It is mystifying to one who has seriously studied the social, economic and political origins of Ameerica as to why it is difficult for many social scientists to acknowledge the objective nature of American society. Critics of the colonial thesis have advanced several models or paradigms that seemingly explain the American ethic. Among those theories which they have advanced are the cultural pluralist model, the integrationists assimilationist model and others. None of these theories are valid. Although well intentioned, their actions have played directly into the hands of the colonizer by dividing and misleading the colonized, thereby strengthening the hold of the colonizer on the oppressed. It is far easier to dominate a colonized group that cannot agree to the characteristics of their oppression than it is to dominate an organized oppressed people who are under the leadership of an aware elite who fully understands the realities of their situation.

The positions taken by these scholars are mystifying because in all areas, with the exception of race relations, they insist upon scholarly objectivity. They will not face up to the fact that America was founded on the principle of domination by the Western Europeans over people of color. The concept is explicit in the constitution of this country. The issues were debated by the founding fathers and after

23

due deliberation, the vigorous disapproval of abolitionist notwithstanding, the principle of domination was incorporated in this document as an expression of the ethos and normative values of the newly founded country.

Few countries in the world have faced the racial question as squarely as the American people and very few societies have as clearly defined the role that people of color are to play in their society as the Americans. Regarding this point, John Hope Franklin informs:

"It is only natural that slavery should have become an important consideration in the constitutional convention. In the heated debates over representation in the Congress, the question arose as to how the slaves would be counted. Most of the northern delegates could regard slaves in no light except as property and thus not deserving any representation. The Georgia and South Carolina delegates were loud in their demands that Negroes be counted equally with the whites. Gouverneur Morris declared that the people of Pennsylvania would revolt on being placed on an equal footing with slaves, while Rufus King of Massachusetts flayed slavery in a firey speech and condemned any proposal that would recognize slavery in the constitution. The three-fifths compromise that was finally written into the constitution was perhaps satisfactory to no one, but it demonstrates clearly the strength of the preslavery interests at the convention. It was inserted in Article I, Section 2, and reads as follows:

Representatives and direct taxes shall be appointed among the several states which may be included within this Union, according to their respective numbers, which shall be determined by adding to the whole Number of free Persons, including those bound to Service for a term of years, and excluding Indians, not taxed, three-fifths of all other persons."[4]

If the foregoing is not sufficient to stifly critics of the colonial analogy, Chief Justice Taney's majority opinion in Dred Scott vs. Sanford, surely erases all doubts as regards to the status of blacks in America. Justice Taney writes:

"The question is simply this: can a Negro, whose ancestors were imported into this country and sold as slaves, become a member of the political community formed and brought into existence by the Constitution of the United States, and as such become entitled to all the rights and privileges, and immunities, guaranteed by that instrument to the citizen ..."

"The words 'people of the United States' and 'citizens' are synonymous terms and mean the same thing. They both describe the political body, who, according to our republican institutions, form the sovereignty, and who hold power and conduct the government through their representatives. They are what we familiarly call the 'sovereign people,' and every citizen is one of this people, and a constituent member of this sovereignty. We think not, and that they are not included, and were not intended to be included, under the word 'citizens' in the Constitution, and can, therefore, claim none of the rights and privileges which that instrument provides for and secures to citizens of the United States. On the contrary, they were at that time considered as subordinate and inferior class of beings, who had been subjugated by the dominant race, and whether emancipated or not, yet remained subject to their authority, and had no rights or privileges but such as those who held the power and the government might choose to grant them ..."[5]

The last sentence of the above quote is crucial in the study of race relations in America. It is significant because it reaffirms the principles set forth in the original constitution as the collective will of the American people. In this connection, John Hope Franklin's comments regarding arguments pertinent to the adoption of Article I, Section 2 of the Constitution has given additional validity as an expression of the collective will. It should be noted that the primary concern of the advocates of the three-fifths rule was that they should not be reduced to the status of the slaves. It is highly significant that they would not entertain the idea of elevating the slave or free blacks to their status.

Some may be inclined to believe that there is very little difference between being reduced to a level of equality or raised to a level of equality, but the difference is far from an exercise in semantics. There is a qualitative difference in the two propositions that bears directly on the question of dominance, namely the colonizer-colonized relationship. Implicit in this nation's framework of government is the idea that there is a dominated group that should remain in a subordinate status to the dominant political and social order. In the case of American society, the subordinate group is explicitly described in terms of racial characteristics.

Judge Taney's infamous ruling carried the description of the class that is subordinated. He refers directly to that class of persons whose ancestors were Negroes of the African race. We can safely conclude that the exclusion of other third-world people from his directive is due to the nature of the case before him at the time. That Chief Justice Taney expressed the will of the American people cannot be denied in view of the history of race relations in America. Clearly, Third-World people in the United States enjoy only those rights and privileges that the people and government choose to grant them.

Social scientists, historians and legal scholars argue that much of the preceding is true, but point out that in the twentieth century there have been many Court rulings and considerable legislative action in an effort to nullify the effects of this decision. It is concerned that liberal whites and blacks have worked together to mitigate the oppression of the masses of third-world people, but the general thrust of their actions has been to reinforce Judge Taney's rulings. The rights and privileges enjoyed by third-world people, whether granted by judicial decree, legislative action or executive orders, are those specifically granted by the dominate race (colonizer) to the subordinate race (colonized) in the context of the collective will to which Judge Taney was speaking. Although a Civil War was fought partly to eradicate slavery and constitutional amendments adopted to guarantee equality, the realities of domination and oppression are prevalent in American society.

The proposition that one group can grant others the privileges of fair employment, fair housing (effect on mobility), equal education and many other privileges, presupposes that one group is conscious of its dominance and has a legitimate right to specify those rights that a subordinate group may exercise. The same principle applies to the restriction of rights and privileges in presupposing that the dominate group has the right to restrict the rights of the subordinate group when it is perceived that these restrictions will be in the best interest of those in power. We find therefore, in regard to American citizens of color, they are simultaneously granted privileges in some areas, restricted from exercising certain privileges, and treated with benign neglect regarding other matters. However, they are never considered to have inalienable rights that cannot be violated.

25

Critics of the colonial analogy and advocates of the assimilationist model, it seems to me, have a herculean task ahead of them if they are to rationalize the objective facts of American life in the terms of their models. As Alber Memmi has made abundantly clear, "It is the colonized who is the first to desire assimilation and it is the colonizer who refuses it to him. How can the colonizer or dominate racial group be expected to accept assimilation fully? Assimilation would destroy the colonizer or dominate group as such."[6] In order that there will be no substantial changes in the power balance between the races in America, racism was institutionalized to perpetuate this dichotomy between white America and third-world people.

It can be readily recognized that internal colonization in America is historical in its development, and that it exists as an expression of the will of the dominant race. The founding fathers of the United States have been applauded for their foresight in drafting the Constitution. Many newer countries have adopted its principles, incorporating them into their constitutions as an expression of the inalienable rights of all mankind. A closer analysis of this document and the intent of its authors reveals that its principles can be and have been used to justify the actions of the most oppressive and infamous regimes in the history of the world. A facist in World War II Germany could find moral justification in the American Constitution for their social excesses, just as the racist government of South Africa or Rhodesia can find similar justification for the oppressive actions of their actions of their governments in this document. Further justification and support can be found in the attitudes and practices of the American colonizing group.

Exponents of the assimilationist model fail to take into account the fact that assimilation was intended for the white races of Western Europe only. When large migrations of Jews, Eastern and Southern Europeans occurred in the early part of this century and after the later migration of blacks in large numbers to the urban centers, the urban power structure removed the primary vehicle for political assimilation of ethnic groups into the decision making process of the urban community. That vehicle was ward politics and the unreformed city government. The trend toward reformed city government took place in most communities after the assimilation of most ethnic groups from Northern and Western Europe and immediately preceding the influx of blacks to large urban centers. Prior to this time, the strong mayoral form of government with strong ward leaders capable of delivering the votes of their ethnic wards led to the seizure of many of the functions of local government by successive waves of immigrant minorities. From this power base, state government and the governmental bureaucracies were forced to cater to the will of these immigrant minorities in an effort to obtain political support. However, this pattern was not to be the case for black Americans.

In areas that maintained the unreformed city government, there are early indications of black political organizations and political mobility. Oscar DePriest was elected alderman from the densely populated South Side of Chicago in 1915. DePriest was elected to the National House of Representatives in 1958. Edward A. Johnson was sent to the State Assembly in New York in 1917 as black political strength grew in areas with unreformed city governments. In areas of the country where blacks did not migrate in overwhelming numbers, i.e., cities where blacks do not represent a near majority of the population, the process of gaining political power was impeded in reformed city governments.[7]

When black Americans arrived in significant numbers and Eastern and Southern Europeans arrived in the core cities, apparently some white urbanites decided that the ward system was too corrupt and expensive to maintain. Blacks were forced into certain restricted areas to live and under the prevailing system, their members

26

would demand representation in the decision making process of the communities. The danger which the presence of highly populated black areas posed was that urban power and control of the administrative and police apparatus of these urban reservations could slip from the control of the colonizers into the hands of the colonized.

Swift action was initiated to counteract a possible shift in political, social and economic power from the hands of the colonizer to those of the subordinate race and other ethnic groups of lower-status. The reformed city government was quickly justified by politicians, political scientists, reformers and others as a means of eliminating the spoils system in local governments. These same politicians who, a generation preceding, utilized this method of assimilation, and who had new vested interests, were the first to deny it to the black newcomers. The results were that under the guise of removing city administration from the pressures of partisan politics in order that it may operate with greater efficiency, many communities changed to a weak mayor, strong city manager form of government. Oakland, California is one of these cities.

This reformed city government arrangement eliminated the ward system or in some cases, introduced the one ward system to the cities. Politicians were required to run for office on a city wide basis, thereby neutralizing the effects of the black vote. The lack of strong ward leadership effectively eliminated any strong political activism on the part of the colonized blacks. By blocking their entrance to the political machines at the grass root level, their fate was left in the hands of an at-large electorate that was to continue to rule the black areas from the distant suburbs. The support, financial and otherwise, that is necessary for one to compete in a city-wide election was effectively denied to the members of the colonized minority, and thus their subordinate status was reaffirmed. Assimilation was thereby procedurally denied by the majority community.

Although the situation has changed in some degree in recent years, the movement to deny the urban minority communities the right to participate in the decision making processes of urban communities has been perpetuated. Several communities that have large minority populations of color are in the process of restoring to regionalism. This movement is a thinly disguised method designed to preserve the control of the power of local governments in the hands of local ruling elites. Already some local communities have contracted regional water districts, electricity districts, park districts, pollution districts, fire districts and others in an effort to effectively emasculate the powers of local city halls. In the event that the minorities and liberal whites should gain control of local governments, they will find that they are restricted in their action by these regional compacts, and that the power that existed a decade ago in these governments will remain in the hands of the white community through these regional compacts.

Advocates of assimilation and the immigrant analogy fail to take into account the variant philosophical positions of the colonized. Although historically it appears that assimilation is first desired by the colonized there are limits as to the price they will pay to achieve this position. In recent years, colonized blacks have been seriously considering the negative effects of assimilation or acculturation that deny their distinctive cultural heritage. There are indications that the trend toward migration to large northern or western cities by minorities or color is stabilizing. The continued rejection of assimilation by the dominant community forces the colonized to look inward or to seek alternate methods of achievement in this society. Third World people are constantly defining their role in relation to the dominant community, and this continual re-definition is necessary for the survival of the colonized community.

The situation of blacks in Newark, New Jersey, exemplifies the typical manipulation of the actions of whites and the economic power structure when there is a probability that blacks will control the local political apparatus. Joseph M. Confortis indicates the following:

"For the city's blacks the growing political activism that began in 1965 was becoming irrelevant as funds diminished; a functionally illiterate generation of youth was graduating from school; a 150-acre site was being surveyed for condemnation to make way for a new medical school; the board of education had retained a white secretary and a white majority on the board itself, in a city with a 75 percent black student body; and municipal elections had just returned whites to office in a city that was at least 50 percent black, but could count only two (out of nine) black councilmen and no blacks in strategic administrative positions in the city's government. Further, whatever hopes blacks may have had of inheriting the city were dampened by the wholesale flight of whites and the economic interest they represented."[8]

Black Culture and Assimilation in the Context of Internal Colonialism

In the past few years, several prominent social scientists in the field of race relations have rejected the assimilationist model in deference to the internal colonialist model. It is unclear at this point whether the acceptance is based on their own perception of the realities of the world, or whether they are responding to the cries of the oppressed. For many years, blacks have listened to a distant drum beat, one which the colonizer has chosen to ignore. The colonizers have been secure in their superior technological society, assuming that all who could associate with it would want to assimilate into it. They were surprised and angered by groups among the colonized who denounced those in control and openly challenged them in addition to their superiority.

The motives behind this challenge were not comprehensible to those in authority. They could not understand why blacks would even want to agitate against the status quo. In their perception, blacks were achieving at all levels, their logic is based on perceptions such as: the standard of living in America among black people is far superior to that of any nation where there are people of color. How could it be that black Americans would denounce these wonderful things that America offers them? Many have Cadillacs, there is a black United States Senator and a black on the United States Supreme Court. What else could blacks possibly want? Some of the colonizers would reply that they are simply ungrateful, and the more you give them, the more they want.

This posture is clearly a reflection of the arrogance of the dominant culture. However, it did serve to prod some social scientists into taking another look at the various existing theories pertaining to race relations. America depicted as a melting pot had disintegrated before their eyes, and with its demise, predictions of racial harmony and assimilation were utterly destroyed. They were thereby forced to look at the racial situation inductively in order to find answers to the social phenomena that they were witnessing. Because the nation appeared to be on a course of monumental racial conflict, in an effort to preserve the stability of the normative social order, social scientists were compelled to take a look at the world from the viewpoint of the colonized.

It is significant that the leaders and participants in much of the turmoil of the past decade, were from the group of colonized who had benefited most from the colonized situation. It has been clearly established that the major social disturbances of rebellions of the past decade (although in many cases spontaneously ignited), were usually led by the working and middle class Afro-Americans who had become frustrated by their lack of social and economic mobility.

In the context of internal colonialism, cultural nationalism is usually the last refuge of a colonized bourgeoisie. The colonized bourgeoisie turns to cultural nationalism when assimilation fails. The masses of colonized peoples do not need this cultural prop because they have been socialized to a state of subjugation which did not permit them to even hope to enter the colonizer systems as partners. Since there were no major efforts on the part of the colonizer to include the colonized masses into the established socio-political system, they became the keepers and protectors of the native culture. They clung to the residuals of African culture such as Voodoo, food and music. It is to the colonized masses that the bourgeoisie must turn when their aspirations are rejected. It is the colonized bourgeoisie that has a crisis of identity.

Robert Blauner addresses this point in a comparison of immigrant and black ghettos:

"Whereas the immigrant ghettos allowed ethnic culture to flower for a period, in the long term they functioned as way stations on the road to, acculturation and assimilation. But the black ghetto has served as a central fixture of American racism strong resistance of assimilation of black people. Thus the ghetto's permanence had made it a continuing crucible for ethnic development and culture building ..."

"Yet it was the same racist society that willy-nilly encouraged the development of the Afro-American culture. Blocking the participation of black people in the dominant culture meant that the human need for symbols, meaning and value had to be met elsewhere. There must have always been many who found these meanings in 'separatist' ethnic forms: there were others who sought them in the attempt to enter fully into the larger culture ..."

"Racist social relations have different cultural consequences from class relation, and therefore black culture cannot be forced into the procrustean bed of lower class culture in the way that Marxist at one and some liberal social scientists today have wanted to reduce race relations to class relations ..."

"Of course, black culture accepts the American emphasis on money, the material accoutrements of affluence, and many other goals--probably including even the suburban life style. In its racist dimension, America excludes people of color and maintains the ghettoized communities that provide fertile ground for ethnicity, while in its inclusive, mass homogenizing dimension America beckons blacks and all others to identify with its material and ideal symbols and to participate in at least the middle levels of consumption and life styles."[9]

Initially, the return of the black middle class to the native culture is perceived as one would receive a prodigal son, although it is recognized that this return will be of a temporary nature. Initially it will have the effect of unifying the black masses with the black intelligensia who have incorporated many of the dominant culture's ideals and values which cannot be easily cast aside. The black middle class finds during this period, that most of the native culture is foreign to them because it cannot be adopted to a dynamic process of modernization that is a part of the colonization process. In other words, the middle class existence can be justified only in terms of the colonizer's culture and the colonial model that defines their social and economic roles as intermediaries. Therefore, the return of the black middle class will be temporary because of the fundamental contradictions in the cultures of the colonizer and the colonized.

The concept of internal colonialism posses the problem of domination. How are the oppressed socialized to their subordinate positions? What is the mechanism of social control that permits the dominate society to rule effectively and hold in subjugation millions of people of color? There has been considerable study of these significant points. Generally, social scientists have concluded the role of the colonized elites are crucial in the terms of social control. Indeed, this class is seen as a cultural, political and economic conduit between the colonizers and the colonized.

The middle class's perceptions of their roles is of importance in the process of interaction with the colonized masses and the white majority population.

Table 4

ROLES OF INTERMEDIARIES

Reply to: "Some may define your role in view of your position as an intermediary between the white and black communities. How do you define your position?"

	Traditional Elites (percent)	New Urban Elites (percent)
Role as an intermediary	63	51
Not an intermediary	31	23
No response	6	26
Total	100	100

The traditional and new modernizing elites have a sense of leadership in situations where there are racial interests. This general consensus among this group of people obviously leads to a class and leadership consciousness that separates them from the black masses in terms of their role definition. However, this class difference should not be generalized as a difference in the objectives of the two classes because the dynamics of internal colonialism in America has racial aspects that limits the operation of the black middle class as well as the black lower classes. The elimination of racism and the modernization of black Americans are the goals of both segments of the middle class. This aspect of the society is understood by the intermediaries.

The role of the colonized middle class which he refers to as the national middle class in a colonial situation, has been described as follows by Franz Fanon:

"The national middle class discovers its historic mission: that of intermediacy."

30

"Seen through its eyes, its mission has nothing to do with transforming the nation; it consists prosaically of being the transmission line between the nation and a capitalism, rampant though camouflaged, which today puts on the mask of neo-colonialism. The national bourgeoisie will be quite content with the role of the western bourgeoisie's business agent, and it will play its part without any complexes in a most dignified manner. But this same lucrative role, this cheap-Jack's function, this meaness of outlook and this absence of all ambition symbolizes the incapability of the national middle class to fulfill its historic role of bourgeoisie. Here, the dynamic, pioneer aspect, the characteristics of the inventor and of the discoverer of new worlds which are found in all national bourgeoisies are lamently absent. In the colonized countries, the spirit of indulgence is dominant at the core of the bourgeoisie; and this is because the national bourgeoisie identifies itself with the western bourgeoisie, from whoever it has learnt its lessons. It follows the Western bourgeoisie along its path of negation and decadence without ever having emulated it in its first stages of exploration and invention, stages which are an acquisition of the Western bourgeoisie whatever the circumstances. In its beginnings, the national bourgeoisie of the colonial countries identifies itself with the decadence of the bourgeoisie of the west. We need not think that it is jumping ahead; it is in fact beginning at the end. It is already senile before it has come to know the petulance, the fearlessness, or the will to succeed of youth."[10]

Those members of the colonized middle class who are identified with the concept of blackness or negritude realize that this identification is a transitory state in the evolution of the oppressed. They perceive that they must motivate and lead the colonized beyond their negative cultural state of being. They tend to give dynamic impetus to other members of the oppressed who will, in turn, fill the roles abandoned by the traditional elites who have been thrust into roles of intermediaries.

Hean-Paul Sartre comes very close to putting the concept of negritude into its proper prospective. He said that it is one term in a dialectric progression the ultimate of which would lead to full independence and to the synthesis of races:

"But there is something more important: The Negro, as we have said, creates an antiracist racism for himself. In no sense does he wish to rule the world: He seeks the abolition of all ethnic privileges, wherever they come from: He asserts his solidarity with the oppressed of all colors ..."

"In fact, negritude appears as the minor term of a dialectical progression: The theoretical and practical assertion of the supremacy of the white man is its thesis; the position of negritude as an antithetical value is the moment of negativity. But this negative moment is insufficient by itself, and the Negroes who employ it know this very well; they know that it is intended to prepare the synthesis or relization of the human society without races. This negritude is the root of its own destruction, it is a transition and not a conclusion, a means and not an ultimate end."[11]

Sartre understands the transitory nature of negritude, which was of great concern to Franz Fanon. However, Albert Memmi's characterization of Fanon is debatable, it cannot be denied that Fanon was one of the foremost proponents of negritude and Fanon took exception with those who placed limitations of this concept.

31

"Inside the political parties, and most often in offshoots from these parties, cultured individuals of the colonized race make their appearance.
For these individuals, the demand for a national culture and the affirma-
tion of the existence of such a culture represent a special battleground
... Confronted with the native intellectual who decides to make an aggressive response to the colonialist theory of pre-colonial barbarism, colonialism will react only slightly, and still less because the ideas developed
by the young colonized intelligentsia are widely progressed by specialist
in the mother country ... The passion with which native intellectually
defend the existence of their national culture may be a source of amaze-
ment; but those who condemn this exaggerated passion are strangely apt to
forget that their own psyche and their own selves are conveniently shel-
tered behind a French or German culture which has given full proof of its
existence and which is uncontested."[12]

Implicit in Fanon's discussion is the black culture that in many aspects is in
opposition to Western European culture and which the colonizers have insidiously
tried to destroy as a means of domination. On the other hand, this culture has
survived and become the refuge for the black intelligensia and the oppressed masses.
Further, consciousness of black culture becomes an instrument for the liberation of
the oppressed. However, Fanon's analysis does not properly take into account black
culture after liberation. Black nationalism and culture is the end of his dialectic.
He fails to understand as Sartre did, that black liberation is but one step in the
liberation of all the oppressed people and not until this is accomplished, can one
be absolutely free of domination.

Any description of black culture in the internal colonial situation that does
not take into account the characteristics of the dominant culture is incomplete and
invites the label of romanticism. In the colonial relationship, both the colonizer
and the colonized interact and cultural diffusion is the result. This cultural
interaction between people of African ancestry and Western European ancestry has
been continuous in the Western Hemisphere over a period of four hundred years.

The love-hate relationships of the colonizers and the colonized are partly the
result of the realization that there are desirable qualities in the historical culture of both groups, although the racist colonizers and oppressed militants are
quick to deny this point. Each group is transformed to some extent by this relationship. For the oppressed, the colonizer's superior technology is envied and
copied. Additionally, the oppressed in many instances, adopt the western concept
of religion, marriage, divorce, work ethics, time and many other cultural norms
while clinging to African residuals.

This cultural diffusion is not limited to internal colonialism. It is almost
universally true that where colonial powers have had contact with a different culture, the indigenous culture has been somewhat transformed by the confrontation.
If we look at the history of developing countries around the world, we would find
that most of their political systems in some degree are a direct offshoot of Western
European systems. In America, the institutions of higher education have large
numbers of foreign scholars, eager to learn about American institutions so that
they can return to their home lands and institute changes in their political systems to make them more viable in a western dominated international society.

Because man's knowledge is expanding as he gains more and more control over
his environment, it is necessary that dynamic cultures constantly change in an effort

to cope with the new realities of everyday life. When different cultural groups are in contact with each other for an extended period of time, both cultures are somewhat transformed. Certainly, no culture worthy of surviving can be based on negativity. Ideally, any culture should be willing to incorporate new ideas that enhance their people while retaining those characteristics that make it distinctive regardless of the source of those ideas.

Nationalism must be seen as a tool in the black man's battle for liberation, but it is only one necessary step in many. If not viewed from this perspective, then cultural nationalism in the extreme becomes a goal in itself and detracts the attention of the oppressed from other sources of oppression such as, political, economic and racist oppression. It has been demonstrated that in some instances where the colonizer has voluntarily left the colony and the colonized were granted independence without violence, their departures have been resisted by elements of the colonized. In these situations the colonized perceive their economic or political viability threatened by the withdrawal of the colonizer and they resist unilateral abrogating the colonial relationship. The colonizer-colonized relationship is one of interdependence. When either group perceives a beneficial dependence on the other, discontinuance of the relationship will be resisted. The colonial system has differential effect on the colonized and often creates a group among them who identifies with and have a vested interest in maintaining the colonial relationship.

It should be the task of the colonized intelligensia and middle class opinion makers to lead in such a way that the exaggerated passions of cultural nationalism does not become a liability in the overall struggle. Cultural domination is only a means whereby the colonizer can exploit others economically and politically. There are indications that the colonizer will willingly relinquish his control in this area as long as the political and economic balance remains unchanged.

Harold Cruse, noted black scholar and author, asserts that the Afro-American problem is fundamentally a cultural one. He writes:

"From all this, it is clear that assimilation tendencies in the outlooks of Afro-American intellectuals, artists, writers, etc., have made our cultural problem a very complex one. It is for this reason I believe the Negro problem in the United States to be primarily a cultural question--yet it is precisely the cultural side of the question which is most overlooked and neglected. On the cultural phase of our American existence, we find keys to questions of identity, cultural values expressed in group institutional forms, standards of judgment in literature, art, music, dance, drama, poetry and social historiography."[13]

Cruse, a former marxist, exemplifies the intellectual bourgeoisie who has turned nationalist. His conception and understanding of culture is frustrating when viewed from the colonial perspective and his lack of perception of Afro-American culture is largely due to the use of faulty definitions. For example, he states: "When one speaks of a culture in the creative sense, one thinks of art, literature, music, drama, dance, language, skills and crafts, architecture, etc., and when one thinks of liberation of oppressed peoples, one assumes a rebirth and a flowering to that peoples' native 'culture' as a corollary of the rise to independence."[14] Cruse's understanding of culture entails only its outward manifestations. The culture of a people regardless of whether or not it is a revolutionary society, resides in the manner they choose to adjust to their environment, that is, their habits, traits, traditions, religion, mores, values and their world view.

There is a distinctive Afro-American culture. It is a culture that flowers in the ghettos of America, and includes residuals of the native African culture with a heavy infusion of Western European culture. After over three hundred years in Northern America and in constant contact with white Americans, many of the customs of the dominant culture have been infused in the colonialized groups. Among these values that have been diffused are: Christianity, the Protestant ethic, and distributive justice.

It is apparent that for the Afro-American to deny the American part of the heritage simply because he cannot accept these aspects of American culture that are revolting, such as racism and domination, would give a false picture of the nature of the Afro-American. The Afro-American is not African and of course, he has never been incorporated into the mainstream of the political, social, and economic structure of American society except in a very limited supportive way. The Afro-Americans' positions outside of the American mainstream leaves them in a situation wherein they can assume the stance of Malcom X which says, "We don't think your civilization is worth the effort of any black man to try to integrate into."[15] Many blacks may willingly refuse to integrate into the American society, but integration is a moot point because as this study demonstrates, significant numbers of the colonized are no longer interested in this method of resolving the racial problem. Further, integration presupposes acceptance by the group being integrated into. There has been no indication that the dominant society wishes to absorb the minority, colonized peoples of color.

The notions of integration or non-integration bring us face to face with this problem of Afro-American culture. As Cruse intimates, integrationist organizations such as the National Association for the Advancement of Colored Peoples, Congress on Racial Equality, the National Urban League and the Southern Christian Leadership Conference, mitigate against Afro-American Nationalism, especially the cultural aspects of nationalism. On the other hand, extreme separatist organizations such as the Nation of Islam and other sects are in opposition to the older established civil rights organizations.

The new nationalist movement seemingly is founded ideologically on a continuum between the two principal points of view. There can be no doubt, however, regarding one point, that is, the nature of the integrationist organizations are such that they inspire little confidence in the black masses except on emotional issues. The organizations that dominate the integrationist movements are overwhelmingly middle class with little, if any, participation by the masses in the decision making processes. The nationalist organizations seemingly have a great deal of appeal to some elements of the masses who are otherwise devoid of political and social mobility.

Cruse further indicates that in the civil rights struggle, the racial integration movement is being led by the black middle class, composed of lawyers, professionals, educators, ministers, public office holders, politicians and others. He sees their aims as follows:

"For the middle classes, the civil rights drive is aimed at achieving much more than mere 'civil rights' for the masses. The prime motivations of the bourgeoisie leaders of this movement are selfish class interests, because the main objective of the Negro middle class is a status and a social position approximating as closely as possible that pre-eminence enjoyed by the great Anglo-American middle class. Practically everything in Negro life today is being subordinated to that aim, including ideas on art and culture (such as they are)."[16]

Cruse's comments on the black middle class are valid in that in a colonial situation this class is a necessary tool because it is essentially the mechanism of control between the colonizer and the colonized. However, their performance and function in the American experience context exceed the conduct necessary to carry out this function. They have taken on many of the decadent trappings which have been cast off by the colonizers. As the white middle class discards fraternities and sororities, the black middle class fraternities and sororities have experienced phenomenal growth. Black cotillions are more popular among this class today than ever before. Secret fraternal and social clubs flourish in the black community. These factors among others have alienated the black middle class from the masses and in doing so have produced a cleavage that will be difficult to abridge in a colonial society.

This cleavage between the black middle classes and the alienated masses is a direct result of the internal colonialist situation. While holding the colonized masses in subjugation, the colonizer will often use the attributes and symbols of culture as a device to dominate the colonized group by permitting enough social mobility to create a facade of full participation in the dominant culture for a select colonized few. There are always those willing to deny and ridicule their heritage at the expense of their own colonized group in exchange for identification with the dominant group. In many ways, the black middle class under scrutiny is probably the most resistant group, in the colonial situation, black or white, to the establishment of a distinctive black culture.

The resistance on the part of the black middle class stems from the realization that the establishment of a distinctive black culture would undermine part of the basis of their legitimacy. As envisioned by many Afro-Americans, the black culture would not be based on adaptation to western culture or social class, there would be psychological and social dimensions that would reject the notions of a superior white culture and the desirability to integrate into it.

The foregoing not withstanding, on occasion these middle class integrationists have tackled almost insurmountable odds in their quest for a legitimate role in American society. Their courage in facing up to racist manifestations of the colonial system has helped to preclude the development of manifest hostility among the masses, and is often misunderstood by the lower classes. Most Afro-Americans applaud their achievements in the fields of civil rights, legislation and in the courts. Although much of their activity is considered as self serving by some, there is no denying that there has been some residual positive effects for the masses.

Many blacks remember these both black and white, who gave their lives or suffered great humiliation and hardship to further the causes of racial progress. The courage of Martin Luther King in his fight to integrate the institutions in the South is remembered with pride, and many blacks can still remember the attorneys for the National Association for the Advancement of Colored Peoples, black and white, who braved the lynch mobs of the South to fight for the legal rights of clients who were otherwise denied proper legal representation. However, in several regions of the country, the closer blacks came to equalizing their position in relation to whites, they received additional resistance from the majority community, especially in ethnic areas of the North in housing, jobs and school integration.

Coalitions in Pursuit of Integration

Those who espouse the tenets of integration have made several serious attempts to form coalitions in an effort to change the social-political structure of this country. Lerone Bennett, Jr., in regards to these efforts has noted that:

"Nobody in this country has tried harder and longer to cooperate with other people on a non-racial basis."

"No other group in this country has sought integration for so long with so little help from the government, from the church, from labor and from other men and women."

"Over and over again, year after year, century after century, Ethiopis has stretched forth her hand to poor whites, rich whites, liberal whites, intelligent and illiterate whites."

"And at this crucial moment, while the storm clouds are gathering, we have a mandate from all the martyrs and victims to take counsel with ourselves and our yesterdays in order to chart a course for tomorrow."

"For, as Santayana has said, men who cannot remember the past are condemned to repeat it."[17]

Bennett writes bitterly of the efforts of the leaders of the black race in America to achieve equality and dignity. As Memmi indicated, the history of their struggles are typical of colonized people. Bennet, in lamenting the black man's struggle, fails to indicate an understanding of the colonial perspective. He fails to understand that coalitions are doomed to failure because in a colonial situation, integration would eliminate the colonizer as surely as it would eliminate the colonized. Viewed from the colonial perspective, it is highly unlikely that the colonizers would willingly give up their positions of privilege. Certainly, the history of American race relations validates this point, however, the colonized bourgeoisie in this study indicates a certain doubt as to the ability of blacks and liberal whites to reverse the oppression of the colonizer. The date in Chapter 4, substantiates this conclusion. Nonetheless, Bennett has accurately described several attempts of blacks to form coalitions. They are:

"The first strategy revolved around an attempt to create a substantial coalition with the power structure, with rich and upper-class whites, with the philanthropists and entrepreneurs and power brokers. This strategy was and is based on the idea that the rich and powerful are not in direct competition with blacks for goods and services. Hence according to this argument, the powerful can afford to be more generous, more charitable."

"The second attempt to create a black and white coalition has revolved around middle-class white progressives or liberals, who are more or less committed to the 'American Creed.' This strategy has relied primarily on white liberals or labor, the white church, and interracial affiliates of Jewish Organizations and Protestant and Catholic Churches."

"A third strategy is based on a projected alliance with relatively poor whites. This is the basis of the ancient and enduring dream of black and white labor solidarity."

"The fourth strategy for coalition building in the black community proposes an alliance between blacks and the radical whites of the old and new left."

"The fifth axis of the black quest is the idea of a coalition with other minorities and ethnic groups."

"Sixth and finally, black people have attempted to ally with themselves. By and large, these attempts have been based on the idea that it is impossible to create an external coalition without an internal coalition."[18]

Bennett believes that the blacks most viable coalition is with the alienated, the outcast, the unemployed, the poor and the humiliated of whatever color. Further, he believes that this coalition is not immediately possible, not because of the nationalism of blacks, but because white liberals in general have not dealt with racism. It is evident that both white and black liberals have met and organized from time to time, but each time they have left large alienated constituencies in their respective communities.

It is clear that Bennett sees nationalism as a tool whereby blacks can achieve their ultimate freedom. It is a tool that can unite the colonized blacks into one major force for social change with definable goals. Nationalism becomes a base from which blacks can formulate coalitions with others who are colonized or desire to change the colonial structure. From this perspective, it is the goal of nationalism to establish a viable psychological, political and social base upon which the black community can function to meet its needs.[19]

In the past decade, revolutionaries and militants' insistence that the black minority is a colonized people that was captured on the coast of Africa and held in subjugation by a white majority who have an advanced technology and has gained credence from an increasing array of social scientists and historians. This concept of blacks being internally colonized has historical precedents. Each generation of Afro-Americans has produced separatist with remarkably similar ideas concerning the black American experience. Nationalism and separatism have been among the more persistent notions to be passed on to each generation.

It has also been suggested that the colonized middle-class or bourgeoisie aid in this process of colonization by transmitting to the colonized masses the culture of the colonizer largely through conspicuous consumption and by demonstrating mobility and the utility of the dominant culture. This is largely due to the fact the dynamics of colonization forces the oppressed to participate in their own oppression as a means for survival. The following table addresses black nationalist confinement among the middle class.

Table 5

BLACK NATIONALISM

Reply to: "Is black nationalism a reasonable way to go?"

	Traditional Elites (percent)	New Urban Elites (percent)
Is a reasonable way to go	48	14
Is not a reasonable way to go	20	63
No response	32	23
Total	100	100

The data indicates there is a considerable difference of opinion between the two elites on the question of black nationalism. One of the major differences is the new urban elites who seem to be more inclined toward some form of integration than traditional elites and they reject the tenets of black nationalism overwhelmingly. This may be a result of the differences in their economic base and the fact the new modernizing elites are moderately successful in integrated situations. It is a reflection of the new elite confidence in their ability to bring about change within the existing system. The traditionals who are largely dependent on the black private sector for their income and status are more confident in the ability of Afro-Americans to control their affairs. There is little consensus pertaining to the form nationalism should take. Both groups are divided on whether nationalism within America should have an emphasis on geographical, cultural, economic or political autonomy.

In the American society, the goals of integrationists are middle class goals. Articulated by a small group of blacks with middle class aspirations. Integration has historically meant that black people must give up their identity and deny their heritage. It has also meant that the colonizer was prepared to accept a small number of blacks into a status higher than that of the black masses but lower than the general white population.[20] These practices on the part of the colonizers and the black integrationists have served to further divide the colonized blacks. It is essential that any efforts toward nationalism include the return of these elites to their traditional middle class roles in which they define themselves as leaders of the black masses in an effort to gain some control over their existence.

The obstructions that blacks have experienced in their integration efforts have led many to redefine their roles in relation to the total society, in terms of nationalism. Although gravitating toward nationalism, the concept has not been clearly defined in terms the masses understand. One fact is obvious, to define nationalism in cultural terms may obscure the real objectives of the masses, especially if this cultural definition is essentially a negation of the black's American heritage. Blacks, in general, are no more willing to give up the American part of their culture than they are the African part. Therefore, most movements based primarily on one while ignoring the other, is doomed to be a minority movement in the black community. There can be no solution to the racial problem in America without guaranteeing the integrity of Afro-American culture.

When considering all the goals sought under the auspices of black nationalism, it is apparent that cultural autonomy can be most easily achieved. Although this was not the case in American society, indeed, in many colonial situations, very little effort has been made by the colonizer to co-opt the native cultures. Cultural nationalism poses no serious threat to the political and economic structure of the colonizer and may facilitate exploitation by giving the colonized the semblance of self determination while denying them the political and economic power that makes liberation meaningful.

In spite of Bennett's pessimism in regards to coalitions at this time, it appears that present events will force the blacks to broaden their outlook. While solidifying cultural gains, they will have to look beyond this cultural nationalism in order to develop a means to insure the integrity of their culture. This necessity will lead to political and economic coalitions of other colonized groups.

Recently, we have seen the potential allies of the traditional black elites, organized labor and to some extent the white working class generally support candidates and legislation that are against the best interest of Afro-Americans. This is

illustrated by the hard hat revolt, the alleged backlash that led to a large segment of organized labor support for a conservative national administration in the
National elections of 1972 and the opposition to the Teamsters Union to the viability of the United Farm Workers Union. Admittedly the degree of reaction among
the white working class is somewhat objective. However, the conflict between white
ethnic groups and Afro-Americans in political economic and social areas has reached
a stage that can no longer be completely ignored. The actions of these whites tends
to support oppression within the context of internal colonialism and around the world
in an effort to protect their position of privilege. While admitting a few blacks
to some of its higher ranks and after supporting most civil rights protests and action from the freedom rides to the 1964 and 1965 Civil Rights bills organized labor
has seemingly reversed its course. The powerful coalitions between labor and Civil
Rights activitists has been destroyed on the twin rocks of racism and self interest.
There is serious doubt at this time that this coalition will ever work together in
the future for effective social-political change.

Logically, it would seem that black labor and civil rights leaders must appre-
ciate the commonality of interest of all of the people who are oppressed and held
into colonial subjugation by the American system. A recognition of this commonality
of interest would lead black labor into coalitions with such organizations as the
United Farm Workers, Native American and Asian-American groups who are struggling
for a measure of control over their lives and human dignity. However, the colonizer
will not willingly surrender any of his privileges in this area.

In a colonial situation, change rarely occurs unless it is advantageous to the
colonizer. There are a few ways that pressure can be brought upon an oppressor to
effect change. An effective coalition between the oppresses of the central cities
and the rural workers is one way of providing this pressure and would most certainly
be resisted with all the power at the command of the colonizers.

A coalition as is proposed here would give the political and economic leverage
that is necessary to insure the integrity of the several cultures involved. This
would not be an easy task. A coalition of this nature would have to be lead by men
of vision from all of the concerned groups. They would have to rise above petty
jealousies and rivalries that the colonizer traditionally perpetuates among the
oppressed to keep them disorganized. Chief among the colonizers tricks to dominate
is the system of differential rewards. By giving a few rewards to the colonized
and diverting their focus of action to them, then colonizers can deny the substan-
tive goals which the oppressed seek.

Coalitions developed for the achievement of cultural and socio-political goals
are feasible if for no other reason than that the colonizer in the context of internal colonialism in America cannot destroy the colonized without destroying himself. It is true as Sidney M. Wilhelm postulates in "Who Needs the Negro?" that
automation virtually eliminates the necessity of the colonized in American society.[21]

However, the lack of need for the colonized has politicized the oppressed and
brought them to a higher level of consciousness that mitigates against their elimination.

The essential and most crucial point of this discussion is that whereas cultural
integrity for Afro-Americans is essential, it should not be considered as an end in
itself because it will not eliminate colonialism. A good example is the British who
have been noted for their ability to keep cultures intact while holding subjects in

the colonial framework. Regarding this point, Martin Kilson writes: "In-direct
rule is the method of local colonial administration through the agency chiefs who
exercise executive authority. It was applied throughout British colonial Africa
and was, from the standpoint of the metropolitan power's budget, a form of colonialism-
on-the-cheap."[22]

These social theorists who advocate political liberation primarily through cultural means, should proceed with caution for they may find that there is only a very
small constituency behind them. If they could view the world from the prospective
of the masses, they would find that there are other matters of more immediate concern such as food, shelter, clothing, jobs and education. Indeed, it would be necessary to resolve the problems in securing the basic human needs prior to organizing
collective action on the basis of culture. It would be difficult to impress the
ill-fed, ill-clothed, unemployed oppressed of the importance of culture if they are
preoccupied with simply surviving in a colonial situation.

Cultural nationalists are in danger of making the same mistakes that integrationists have made. They are attempting to persuade the black masses into a plan
of action that in many instances they are incapable of understanding. They would be
well advised to discover and to take into account the masses' interpretation of their
situation, prior to endeavoring to place them into any sort of coalition. To proceed on a course of cultural nationalism alone, may force a situation on them that
may lead to a more completely closed colonial situation than the one in which they
currently find themselves.

Racism as an Instrument of Internal Colonialism

Societies in most instances exhibit characteristics that are representative of
the individuals who populate the society. In the United States, we find a society
that is basically colonial. The colonialism is based on racism, both overt and co-
vert. Carmichael and Hamilton indicate that the two forms of racism are closely related. The first form consists of individual whites acting against individual blacks.
The second form is characterized as action by the total white community against the
black community.[23]

Many Americans would never commit an act of overt racism but they continue to
support political officials and institutions that would and do institutionally perpetuate racist policies. It is far more subtle, less identifiable in terms of
specific individual acts than a system of overt racism. It is embedded in the respected institutions of government and the society and therefore receives little
condemnation. Institutional racism relies on the active and pervasive operation of
anti-black attitudes and practices.

In his discussion of institutional racism, Charles E. Silberman has concluded
that the tragedy of American race relations is the fact that there is no American
dilemma as postulated by Gunnar Myrdal. He indicates that white Americans are not
torn and tortured by the conflict between their devotion to the American creed and
their actual behavior. According to Silberman, white Americans "are upset by the
current state of race relations to be sure. But what troubles them is not that
justice is being denied but that their peace is being shattered and their business
integrated."[24]

In tracing the history of racism over the past centuries, social scientists and
historians have concluded that racism has both a psycho-historical and cultural dynamic.

Racism is considered a part of the institutions that are derived from Western European or American culture. Therefore, racism is inherent in the culture and all of those who benefit from the culture, if they are white, are racist. This assumption completely subordinates the individual organism to the supremacy of the culture. It does not take into account the individuals and groups who are white who act over and against this cultural variable.

From a psycho-historical perspective Kovel writes:

"Our racial crisis has made us realize that white racism in America is no aberration but an ingredient of our culture which cannot be fully understood apart from the rest of our total situation ... I shall consider our racial dilemma as the product of the historical unfolding of Western culture."[25]

According to other critics of American society, racism is a product of the economic dynamics of an advanced capitalist society. It is a tool of exploitation. Stokely Carmichael sees racism and exploitation as "the horns of the bull that seeks to gore us."[26] However, Carmichael also maintains that even when racism is eliminated, we would still have the problem of exploitation. In this context, racism can be overcome when it becomes dysfunctional to the economic system, and can be replaced by another instrument of exploitation.

Some scholars maintain that in the American colonies, the initial contact of whites with blacks produced very little racist response. Although involuntary servitude was widely practiced, it reflected no color distinction; white and black were both master and servant. But as masters imposed illegal restraints extending the period of labor obligation, servitude became an extremely harsh arrangement and therefore, lost its former attractiveness as a means of covering costs of passage from the Old to the New World.[27] If this logic is followed, we will see that internal colonialism in the New World preceded racism, and racism developed as an adjunct to the economic situation in which the early colonialist found themselves.

Racism in the sense of the immediately foregoing, although economically derivative, later transformed itself. Sidney Wilhelm asserts:

"Once established, racism assumed a determining character in its own right; it must now be taken for a dominant, autonomout social value, which when linked with economic considerations, establishes an elaborate network of social relations between white and black. Economic values no longer impose the color distinction as in the past, but rather out of the initial operation for determinants, they have come to limit the range of Negro-white relationships. For the moment, it will suffice to point out that racism expands and contracts within the restrictions established by economic incentive."[28]

In analyzing racial oppression in the internal colonial situation, Robert Blauner stresses the interaction of both the economic and cultural aspects of racism. Further, he indicates that privilege is the heart of racial oppression and in order to maintain a position of privilege, the majority community has established a large system of social controls based largely upon race. The mechanism of control, "ranging from force and violence, to legal restrictions encompassing cultural beliefs, ideologies, and modes of socio-economic integration, are central to the understanding of oppression."[29] He further indicates that cultural domination may be the most significant mechanism of such racial control.

All of the preceding comments on the various aspects of racism may be valid. Surely, they are at least as valid as black and white radicals' assertions that all whites are racist because white Americans emjoy special privileges in all areas of existence where racial minorities are systematically excluded or disadvantaged.

Racism in its psychological form is necessary before the development of any of its manifestations in the economic system. It is highly unlikely as previously indicated that a change in the economic system would eliminate racism. On this subject Staughton Lynd says, "If the white Americans no longer needed the black Americans' labor, this does not mean that the white American would no longer be racist. On the contrary, as Professor Willhelm views the situation, if the white Americans no longer needed the black Americans' labor, he might then feel free to express his racism fully; not merely to exploit the black American, as in the last 300 years, but to kill him."[30]

Racism has a dynamic that is not dependent upon the economic or political structure of a country. Willhelm feels that in the United States, racism is no pervasive that when there is no longer an economic justification to support some degree of tolerance, the black Americans may very well come to be treated as the American Indian, confined to reservations or perhaps even eliminated.[31]

The Oakland black middle-class's point of view on the extermination of Afro-Americans is as follows:

Table 6

DESTINY OF BLACKS

Reply to: "Sidney M. Willhelm states that the ultimate destiny of the Afro-American is likely to be extermination, not assimilation. What is your reaction to this statement?"

	Traditional Elites (percent)	New Urban Elites (percent)
Likely to be exterminated not assimilated	29	23
Not likely to be exterminated, to be assimilated	40	51
No response	31	26
Total	100	100

Some of the black elites felt that the sheer numbers of black Americans in the various levels of society mitigated against extermination. Others feel blacks are modernizing at a rate that will make them a valuable asset to the American economy rather than a useless appendage. Still others felt that world opinion would not permit programs against black people. One black leader indicated it would be the end of America as a great power and the whites would not risk this action in a world where the interdependency of nations is increasingly based on cooperation with the emerging nations of the third world.

42

The economic and political systems of a country are not causal factors in racism, except perhaps indirectly. Marxist scholars and others have throughout the years attempted to explain racism within the framework of economic systems without much success. Their lack of success is inevitable if they ignore the fact that people make systems, social, political and economic based upon their interpretation of the situation. The concrete units of systems in the social sense are individuals and systems tend to reinforce beliefs and expectations of these units or they are discarded.

In the context of American colonialism, much is made of the fact that racism had economic advantages for white Americans. It would be incorrect to attribute the cause of racism to these economic advantages. Certainly, economic factors encouraged and reinforced racism, but economics was only one of the areas of the white Americal society that benefited from the privileges of racism. It is apparent that once racism was accepted by those who had the power to structure all of the forces in the political and economic order, including in some cases the victims of this exploitation, American society in general reinforced racism. As a result, racism has become institutionalized into almost every fabric of American society.

There is an abundance of evidence to support the contention that before the introduction of slavery into the colonies and before they received any economic or political benefits, Europeans considered people of color to be their subordinates culturally, racially and otherwise. Colonial slavery was an opportunity to benefit from racism. Very little can be understood about racism unless it is clear that people make and perpetuate the systems of society, racist or otherwise. Social definitions usually occur after there is a degree of conflict among those in the society who perceive a vested interest. It should be understood that systems, when they are successful, reinforce the ideas that preceded the systems. Racism had been strongly reinforced in this connection.

Militants, generally, are constantly reminding us that all white people are racist if for no other reason than all whites benefit from the effects of racism. Certainly, all whites may benefit from the exploitation of minorities but the evidence available does not support the notion that all who benefit from this oppression necessarily support it. This contention may have escaped scrutiny entirely if it were not all inclusive, did not allow exceptions and did not stigmatize an entire race of people. It would not warrant discussion if it did not provide the racist elements in the white society who feel that racism is morally justified an argument against those whites who are not racist.

It appears there has been considerable misunderstanding of the definition of racism. In defining racism, Carmichael and Hamilton say: "By 'racism' we mean the predication of decisions and policies on consideration of race for the purpose of subordinating a racial group and maintaining control over the group."[32] A failure to understand this definition of racism has led some into the ridiculous position wherein they indicate that all whites can act only in terms of negative racial imperatives and on the other hand, asking whites to loosen the oppressive bonds that reinforce those imperatives.

Much has been written in an effort to define racism. It is appropriate to point out what is not racism. Racism is not a belief that one culture, religion, society or other factors are superior to another. Racism occurs only when one acts upon these racial determinates in an effort to subordinate, deny human rights, cultural heritage and other rights inherent to a people or the dignity of the individual. Racism can occur either through act or omission. Unfortunately, this definition or explanation does nothing to change the complextion of American society. It is still racist in as much as most of the white Americans support a colonial system that is designed to perpetuate racism, and thereby their position of privilege. Implicit in this explanation is the assumption that all of the members of the majority community are not necessarily racist. There have been many white martyrs in the black man's struggle for liberation.

Some white Americans over act against cultural and racial variables. During the period of the black experience in America, some of them have paid a heavy price for their beliefs that there are certain rights inherent to all Americans. However, a detailed analysis of racism and its effects is beyond the scope of this paper. In discussing the internal colonialist model it is mentioned only because of its function as a system of social, political and economic control.

In America today, the racially oppressed are feverishly working to combat the effects of racism. They are moving on all fronts, politically and economically to find some degree of accommodation with the forces that govern their lives. Some of those who have become frustrated and bitter, have resorted to violence that had often ended in their own demise. At this point in time, the prognosis for race relations in America does not appear encouraging.

For those who advocate separatism, a word of caution: the nature of racism is such that only the degree of separation deemed acceptable by the colonizers will be tolerated. Domination is an important aspects of racism can be eliminated is to make racist practices too expensive for the colonizer to sustain. Withdrawing from the colonizer's economic system may be one of the ways to accomplish this goal, but it is by no means an infallible tactic. The opposite may be true in the sense that it may be more meaningful to move into the political and economic mainstream and transform the oppressive nature of the system. It may be easier for the colonizer to control his colony if all the colonized were to withdraw into clearly defined boundaries. It is also true that there are some advantages for the colonized in a society of their own making. The direction the colonized chooses must be carefully weighed in regards to the best method of achieving their aspirations.

In the internal colonial situation in American society, racism is the primary mechanism of social control. Appeals to the conscience of the racist will not bring about any fundamental changes in the American system. For although privilege is interrelated with racism, if the privileged positions are endangered one cannot be assured that racism would also be eliminated. Racism can only be eliminated by the liberation of the colonized.

People of color in a racist situation must strive to achieve their goals in spite of the pervasiveness of racism. There is a danger in focusing exclusively on racism. It is important that the oppressed do not forget their immediate goal is not necessarily the elimination of racism, but the liberation of the colonized. In this connection, the colonized can ill afford to ignore efforts of others of good will who are working in their behalf regardless of their race or socio-economic status.

Oppressed people seeking control over their destiny will not wait for the eradication of racism to achieve their objectives. The psychological dynamics associated with racism precluded this delay on their part. They will not wait until the colonizer reorders his world in such a way that he no longer objectifies races as being subordinate, and basing all activity upon these interpretations. This revolution in perception necessarily would take a long period of time because the colonizers are

44

not likely to give up their position of privilege based on the easily identifiable reality of race. However, in some cases the colonized can mitigate the effects of racism while assuring that self-determination remains a possibility.

Only after the people of color have achieved some degree of self-determination or power can any in-roads be made into the bastion of racism. In an internal colonial situation, efforts to achieve liberation will be considered "uppity" and will be met with the full force of the racist colonizer, both overtly and covertly. However, in the end, the colonized will settle for nothing less than total liberation.

Therefore, it is apparent that for the colonized, the first objective is power over their destinies. As previously indicated, this liberation is only one major step in the struggle. The second would be a re-ordering of the racist social environment, economic and political systems to eliminate racism and in doing so, to secure the liberation.

Internal Colonialism

In this section, Robert Blauner's Internal Colonialism and Ghetto Revolt will be scrutinized.[33] It is one of the better sociological analysis of the internal colonialist theory. However, there are several points that should be expanded or clarified in order that this theory is placed in the proper perspective of ongoing human interaction and institutionalization. Internal colonialism and the process of colonization as it relates to the broader theory of modernization will be discussed, along with Blauner's contention that the colonial situation in the AFrican context is not analogous to the American blacks' experiences. Basically, it will be argued that his concept should include the American experience. That the essential differences in the two situations revolve around the psychological aspects of colonialism and the fact black Americans are a minority in America. It will be argued that the differences do not render the analogy invalid for sociological inquiry.

Analyzing colonialism without taking into account the world wide model of modernization is the equivalent of analyzing the abdomen without considering the total organism. It can be done, but it leaves the reader with only a capsulized version of the dynamics involved in internal colonialism. Colonialism is a part of the modernization process of the Western World. Immanuel Wallerstein addresses this point as follows:

"The expansion of Europe was part of the modernization of Europe. In the fifteenth century, the Portuguese first reached West Africa, then South and East Africa, to be followed soon thereafter by other European powers. Along one narrow strip alone, the shoreline of the Gold Coast, first were established between the fifteenth and eighteenth centuries by Portugal, England, France, Holland, Denmark, Sweden, and Brandenburg."

"At first, Europeans came mainly to trade and were satisfied with outposts along the shoreline of Africa. This limited interest was reinforced in Southern Africa by a geological fact. The coastal strip was very thin. As soon as one went into the interior, the land climbed rapidly above sea level and penetration became more difficult. The degree of evolution of Europe's economy also set limits on the extent of the trade. The raw materials that Europeans met sought--gold and ivory and slaves--were best provided by African intermediaries."[34]

The black man's contribution to world modernization has been substantiated in the annals of world history. These contributions had effect on the colonized. This contact with the modernization process in America and abroad has left him with a desire to modernize at a rapid rate. It is the possibility of a world of modern, industrialized non-white nations that has frightened colonial rulers and motivated their repressive actions. Modernization is a dynamic force and it is an ineluctable force. To permit it to develop without the strictest controls would jeopardize the tenuous hold of the minority white race on world wide power. This circumstance leads to the perpetuation of the colonial situation and creates conflict whenever the dominant power group perceives an actual or imagined threat to its position. The process of internal modernization will be discussed in greater detail in the following chapter.

Comparative Colonialism

Several authors have pointed out the differences in colonial situations. It is important to note that in terms of effect on human behavior the differences are not as important as the similarities in the colonial analogy. In comparing African colonialism with the American experience, Blauner says:

"It is becoming almost fashionable to analyze American racial conflict today in terms of the colonial analogy. I shall argue in this paper that the utility of this perspective depends upon a distinction between colonization as a process and colonialism as a social economic, and political system. It is the experience of colonization that Afro-Americans share with many of the non-white people of the world. But this subjugation has taken place in a societal context that differs in important respects from the situation of 'Classical colonialism.'"[35]

The dichotomization of the process and the situation are valid in both the African and American context. However, I cannot agree with his characterization of the situations as being basically different for reasons that I will address later in this paper. Further, the process of colonization is many times operative in a society simultaneously with the process of decolonization. This is especially evident in the case of internal colonization where restrictions on institutions affecting the colonized may be lifted and other controls maintained or intensified.

Blauner's definition of classic or traditional colonialism is:

"... Colonialism traditionally refers to the establishment of domination over a geographically external political unit, most often inhabited by people of a different race and culture, where this domination is political and economic and the colony exists subordinated to the mother country ... In difference in power, autonomy, and political status, and various agencies are set up to maintain this subordination ... Classic colonialism involved the control and exploitation of the majority of a nation by a minority of outsiders. Whereas in America, the people who are oppressed were themselves originally outsiders and a numerical minority."[36]

The primary difference between Blauner's definition and the definition of those who believe that African colonialism is analogous to the American situation, is the question of conquered territory and the fact that in America, the blacks constitute a minority group. It is important to note how the oppressed define their own situation. Many American blacks define their position in this country as being one of colonized people. There are even black organizations built upon this premise. Since their actions are based upon this definition, they identify with African culture and they consider their situation to be analogous to the African situation. At least from their perspective, they are indeed colonized people in terms of their perceptions.

It is clear that many blacks, if not most, have never considered America as their home. Indeed, the history of this country indicates very clearly there has always been continuing agitation among blacks for a return to Africa or the establishment of political, cultural and social autonomy in other areas. The rejection of integration by many blacks as a viable means of achieving their aspirations has been rather profound. Evidence of these differences can be seen in the fact that in addition to separatist organizations, blacks for many years have had their own national anthem and many of their spiritual humns are based on the deliverance of a people captured in a foreign land.

The characterization of the black's position in America as a colonized people initially was voiced by the members of the black community. It has been in many instances incorporated into radical rhetoric and is being subjected to sociological inquiry. The news media has advanced to a position where leaders of the community can articulate their viewpoints throughout most of the world in a very short period of time. This accessibility of the media has permitted them to bring to the attention of others their ideas concerning the black's role in society and the role racism, both institutional and psychological, plays in the everyday life of Americans. These viewpoints are not new, but they are firmly rooted in the black-American tradition. It is true, however, that most of the rhetoric remains simply rhetoric because of the ability of the colonizer to deploy his police to his advantage, and the activities of some elements of an internally colonized elite who assist the colonizer in dominating, largely for their own personal gain.

Memmi has clearly indicated that the colonized are the first to seek integration or assimilation. This is certainly true until they obtain a political and cultural consciousness. After this consciousness is acquired, the totality of the colonizer's system if rejected often unreasonably and to the detriment of the colonized. In this stage, the colonized looks inwardly, creating new symbols for social cohesion. In the case of Afro-Americans, blackness became a symbol and black power became the rallying cry of the oppressed.

When the colonized black American leaders realized there was no possibility of assimilation on an equal basis into the established political, economic and social order, it took little effort for them to spur the black masses into an orgy of cultural nationalism rejecting all things associated with the white race, regardless of their utility in nation building and liberation. Suddenly, black middle class students around the country were denouncing traditional liberal institutions as racist and all formal education became unnecessary for black survival. As a matter of fact, they felt that there was nothing a black person could acquire in an educational institution in America that would be functional in the liberation of black people.

Colonialism is defined in the American College Dictionary as "the policy of a nation seeking to extend or retain its authority over other peoples or territories."[37] It can be readily seen that Blauner's definition in part disagrees with the one quoted from the American College Dictionary. It is quite clear also that territorial acquisition is not a requisite condition of colonialism. As previously pointed out by Wallerstein, the intruders first colonized the people of Africa by taking them into slavery and returned later to colonize the land.

Differences in Colonial Situations

To buttress his argument regarding the difference in the two colonial situations, Blauner states , "There has been no formal recognition of differing power since slavery was abolished outside the South."[38] This statement may be factual, however, as late as the second half of the twentieth century, it took Supreme Court decisions to strike down formal discriminatory laws in politics, accommodations and education.

From the perspective of some of the colonized who may not be able, in a state of oppression, to make distinctions between formal and informal recognition of differing power, a situation of colonization exists whether there is a formal recognition of differing powers or if a situation exists where there is exploitation for the benefit of a colonizer through informal exploitical or social arrangements. The colonized will act in terms of their definition of the situation. There are differences in colonial situations that are often dictated by the most appropriate method of exploiting subjects for the benefit of the colonizer group. Necessarily , the dynamics of colonization are effected by the demographic, logistical, political and social situation of the colonized vis-a-vis the colonizer. This has led to different colonizing tactics in different regions of the country as there were different models of colonization in traditional colonial situations.

The point of the discussion is not to argue that there were no differences in the colonial situations, but to suggest that the differences were a matter of degree. The differences are based on the economics of the various colonized areas and the needs of the dominant authority. As previously stated, it seems that the major differences in the two situations were psychological and social. In America, Africans were systematically brainwashed, stripped of their personalities , denied access to traditional leaders and forced to adopt an alien culture. Further, traditional institutions that normally support a people were destroyed and denied to them. This was especially true in the case of African religion and the family , two essential institutions. In Africa, these institutions under colonialism more or less remained intact.[39]

In regard to the argument presented by some scholars pertaining to a difference in the situation that is, the question of blacks in America being a minority and Africans being in the majority, this quantitative face is of little consequence. The controlling variable in colonialism is power not numbers. Students of the subject agree, that the technological superiority of the Europeans gave them dominance in the area of power. This power was used to dominate the black man in both the African and the American situations.

Some social scientists assume that the African colonial situation was uniform on the entire African continent. It is true that there was little difference in the black man's position under this process from colony to colony in Africa and further, there was little overall difference between this position in Africa and in the Western hemisphere; nowhere were the differences great enough to warrant the statement that "seemingly the analogy must be stretched beyond usefulness if the American version is to be forced into this model."[40] Americans operate a colonial system internally with the same institutional restraints that were placed on Africa by Europeans. In both areas, it can be pointed out, that colonization was the result of economic and political decisions, enforced by the coercive military and police powers of advanced technological countries.

48

On the continent of Africa, we find that two major models of colonialism developed, British and French. The British model has been characterized as indirect rule and the French model was considered essentially assimilationist. Wallerstein speaks of the models as follows:

"... In short, British paternalism took the form of pressures to preserve custom, to maintain distance between Britain and Africa. Between Briton and African."

"The paternalism of France took a different form. There was a Jacobin tradition in addition to that of aristocratic romance. During the French Revolution ... and again in the first flush of the Second Republic, in 1848, France granted full rights to citizenship to the inhabitants of the four communes of Senegal, including the right to send a deputy to the parliment in France ..."

"This is what was meant by assimilation. In 1946, France would boast that the official grammarian of the Constitutional Convention was an African ... Leopold Senghor. Neither distance nor racism here; the cultivated African was a deputy of France."

"This, then, is the classic contrast between Africa's two colonial powers, Britain and France: Britain-empirical, commercial, practicing indirect rule, keeping Africans at a distance, verging on racism; France-cartesian in its logic, seeking glory, practicing direct administration, acting as apostle of fraternity and anti-racis. Anyone who travels in both British and French Africa will see the grain of truth in these generalizations. The flavor of life is different; the two colonial powers have produced two different cultures. And yet, anyone who travels there well know the severe limitations of these generalizations.[41]

In America a third model of colonialism evolved. This model was an amalgamation of the above mentioned models. Some observers are misled by the assimilationist aspects of American society today. They believe there was a significant difference between the African and American situations as they pertain to this model. These observers perceive social mobility for blacks in American society. There is mobility in regards to the colonized but vertical mobility in this instance should be compared with the relatively easy assimilation of Western Europeans into the mainstream of American political, economic and social life and the struggle of the Afro-Americans to gain what must be considered, given their length of time in this country, a very limited degree of mobility.

Much has been made of the fact Afro-American constitutes a minority group in the United States. Some conclude that this face creates a significant difference in their situation and the African situation. This point would probably be relevant if we could ignore the fact that until after the Civil War, blacks in America were not Americans. Their status in this country prior to the Civil War and the Thirteenth, Fourteenth and Fifteenth Amendments to the Constitution, was essentially that of a captured people in a foreign land whose citizenship, if any, was with the African tribes from which they were stolen. This predicament was true in spite of the fact many fought and died in wars for this country, helping secure its independence from the British and contributing significantly to its growth.

During the pre-Civil War period, the American model was essentially British in the sense that there was a certain amount of indirect rule and no major assimilationist movement. It is essential to note that during this period, laws and custom strictly regulated the interactions of the races creating as much division as possible. The rule over the blacks in the South was generally enforced by an overseer. In the North, the overseer was usually a minister or black leader appointed by the establishment. There was very little effort on the part of the colonizers to assimilate blacks into the institutional aspects of the majority community. For instance, there was almost no effort to integrate them into the political, social or educational structure of this country in significant numbers.

The Civil War brought about major changes in this model which was analogous to the change in the French colonies after World War I. Americans shifted to a position that was to bring modernization to the blacks. As in the French situation, the premise was that the moral force of this civilization dispensed through education would have more authority in the long run than military force. Therefore, a serious effort was made to educate blacks and transform them into auxiliaries of colonization. This effort manifested itself in the creation of a separate school system in the South and the creation of several small black colleges that emphasized practical trades such as blacksmithing, agriculture and military training. Religion was also taught in these schools as a vehicle of social control. The education was designed to create a functional society and a stratum of blacks who were not dissatisfied with the subordinate nature of their relationships in the larger society.[42]

Further changes in this model indicates that theoretically, blacks were given the right to vote and full citizenship in the way that is almost analogous to the situation in French Africa. In spite of the changes, the colonial powers held the dominant political, economic and military positions. Blacks in America were elected to public offices and some were accorded recognition for their contributions to the American society. As to the character of this change, Coleman, writing in terms of the French-African experience, says:

"The assimilationist character of the educational system in French Africa was a crucial factor in creating an African political elite which identified itself with France and French culture, and insofar as the present generation has been concerned, it has been an elite willing, until recently, to seek political self-realization within the framework of some form of permanent Euro-African relationship."[43]

The foregoing discussion has delineated the characteristics of three separate models of colonialism, however, as previously warned by Wallerstein, we should not be fooled by generalizations, as they have their limitations. However, a close scrutiny of the processes and the different models will reveal many similarities.

The most appropriate conceptual label to explain the conduct of the colonizers and the colonized and to allow for the various differences and similarities would be the term colonial situation. This term is defined as, "by the term colonial situation we simply mean that someone imposes on a given area a new institution, the colonial administration, governed by outsiders who establish rules which they enforce with a reasonable degree of success."[44] This definition is not based upon whether the colonized are a majority or minority population. It is not relevant whether the colonial policy is assimilationist or indirect. The major criterion for the definition is that outsiders are able to enforce their rule.

Urban Riots, Cultural Nationalism and Ghetto Politics

Blauner very accurately analyzes urban riots, cultural nationalism and ghetto politics in the light of the colonization process. In view of the fact that these social movements are pursued at differential rates within the black community affecting relatively small segments of the community at a given time, it may be more appropriate to determine why blacks are not continually rioting in view of their oppression. Why is it that black nationalism remains a minority movement in the black community? Why do referenda, relating to community control of the police, lack substantial support in the black communities? Neither the colonization process or Elkins' arguments, to the effect that dominated people may assume the values of the oppressors, is sufficient to explain this lack of aggressive or radical reaction.[45]

It is only when we consider how blacks define their situation in relation to the modernization process, that the conduct of the colonized group comes into sharper focus. Clearly, blacks are more interested in finding a niche in the ongoing process of modernization and maintaining cultural identity, than they are in the autonomy associated with black nationalism. This autonomy would, at best, achieve a neo-colonial status because any separation would, of necessity, be partially financed by the white colonizers. It is irrelevant whether the money is given or loaned under the rubric or reparations, the financial control is still in the hands of the colonizers. It has been proven that political control is usually allied with finance. Further, the ex-colonizers would control world trade markets and this fact may effectively control the economy of any separate group or developing nation. Black nationalism would be a last resort to be used if all other efforts to live with dignity in the society failed.

On the other hand, if a system of real economic, technological and political integration can be accomplished, while maintaining social and cultural integrity, it would be desirable. In this case, existing educational institutions can be adjusted to meet the needs of the colonized. To what extent the other institutions in America can be modified to meet these needs is questionable. It seems that a majority of the black population feels such modifications are possible. This belief leads to periods of intense racial conflict around a given institution at one point in the modernization process and a decrease in pressure on others. The middle class response to whether integration is possible:

Table 7

INTEGRATION

Reply to: "Is integration possible in America?"

	Traditional Elites (percent)	New Urban Elites (percent)
Integration is possible	66	57
Integration is not possible	20	23
No response	14	20
Total	100	100

Respondents quickly indicated it has been demonstrated in past national crises the American people can work together in spite of their differences. They feel that integration is possible and feasible but they cannot agree on the way to eliminate barriers to integration in the United States. Some point in economic and political action as a solution to this problem. Others place a great deal of emphasis on the education of the black minority and the white majority populations.

The battle in the school systems provides the most eloquent example of the previous point. In this area the focus of a majority of the black community appears to be on quality education with a modification that enhances cultural identity. It has been demonstrated in areas where schools are becoming integrated that blacks overwhelmingly support these actions, if the integration is designed to bring about an improvement in the quality of education. It is only in the instances where blacks are **receiving** an inferior education and have no voice in the process that there are demands for taking over or establishing separate educational institutions. An interesting case in point is District 23 in the Brownsville section of Brooklyn where there has been recent agitation for community control of the schools. The district is virtually all black and Hispanic. In a recent test it had the lowest proportion of pupils reading at or ab ove grade level (13.8 percent) of any district in the New York City system. This district also had the poorest attendance record (80.9 percent).[46]

In areas around the country where blacks can send their children to the schools with high academic ratings, they tend to do so and for the most part avoid schools of the black nationalist minority when they are of low quality. The emphasis is placed on entrance to these schools and the insistance that modifications which meet cultural needs of blacks are established rather than establishing totally separate districts that may perpetuate educational inferiority. The thrust is for the elimination of racism in education. Although I have limited this discussion to a very capsulated version of blacks' position in the area of education (the issue of busing will be discussed in Chapter 4), it can be extrapolated to the realms of economics and politics. It appears that rather than separating fully from the system, blacks are interested in making the system meaningful to them by modifying the existing institutions.

Martin Kilson speaks of rebellion as ameliorating aspects of the use of traditional power.[47] The urban riots in America must be seen in this light, because the thrust of black protest has been with this objective. It has been a demand by an oppressed minority for an opportunity to gain a niche in the ongoing process of modernization and the right to maintain a cultural identity without racism.

When distinctions are based on color, they can be made relatively easily between the colonizers and the colonized. These distinctions are not as easily made when one attempts to base them on recognizable benefits for a colonized situation. This dilemma becomes significant in an internal colonial situation because some among the colonized may willingly give up the trappings of the original culture and submit to various subtle forms of racism in order to achieve a cuperordinal goal such as economic security, political power or prominence. On the other hand as previously indicated, there are those among the dominant race who find oppression on the basis of skin color obnoxious.

Herein lies the mechanism of social control that permits the colonizer to exploit the masses with little need for standing armies to enforce his will. This system of differential rewards reaffirms the position of the traditional bourgeoisie and when necessary, creates a new bourgeoisie to act as intermediaries between the oppressors and the oppressed. After a period of time, in many instances, these elites become identified with the colonial interests that legitimize their social and economic positions. A vested interest in colonialism is established that may lead to this clash with the will of the masses. Usually their tenure of prominence is based on their ability to serve the colonial system and when they become dysfunctional to the system, they are ignored or eliminated.

In speaking of this element in the colonized elite, Fanon indicates that in a colonial situation their interest supercedes their concern for the colonized masses:

"The native intellectual has clothed his aggressiveness in his barely veiled desire to assimilate himself to the colonial world. He used his aggressiveness to serve his own individual interest."

"Thus there is very easily brought into being as kind of class of af-franchised slaves, or slaves who are individually free. What the intellectual demands is the right to multiply the emancipated, and the opportunity to organize a genuine class of emancipated citizens. On the other hand, the mass of the people have no intention of standing by and watching individuals increase their chances of success. What they demand is not the settler's position of status, but the settler's place."[48]

In the context of internal colonialism, this class of emancipated individuals operates in a manner that mitigates against outright revolt on the part of the masses and helps socialize them in terms of Western culture. Too often those social scientists who analyze societies in terms of class analysis, fail to recognize the class distinctions of the colonized. This leads to the belief that the interest of all of the oppressed are the same and that their perceptions and definitions of their situations are similar. Surely, all who perceive oppression among the colonized have a common desire to eliminate it. However, since the colonized are a stratified society, their definitions as to the nature of oppression and the appropriate action necessary to correct this social situation are affected by their relative positions in the social-economic structure of colonialism.

In Chapters 3 and 4 the role of the colonized bourgeoisie will be studied in regards to the modernization process. Further, the roles of the colonized bourgeoisie in a typical American city, Oakland, California and their attitudes toward their roles as intermediaries will be explored. This elite is not only necessary in the maintenance of social control, it is also the vanguard of the modernization process and the actions of this elite in regards to this process has meaning for both the colonizer and the colonized.

REFERENCES TO CHAPTER 2

1. Franz Fanon, <u>The Wretched of the Earth</u> (New York: Grove Press, Inc., 1968)
    pp. 38-40.

2. Ibid.

3. Stokely Carmichael, Oakland Tribune, June 29, 1972, p. 22.

4. John H. Franklin, <u>From Slavery to Freedom</u> (New York: Alfred A. Knopf, 1967)
    pp. 142-143.

5. Robert F. Cushman, <u>Cases in Civil Liberties</u> (Appleton-Century-Crofs, 1968)
    pp. 655-660.

6. Albert Memmi, <u>The Colonizer and the Colonized</u> (Boston: Beacon Press, 1967)
    p. 125.

7. Franklin, op. cit., pp. 524-526.

8. Joseph M. Confortis, <u>Society</u>, October 1972, Vol. 9, No. 10.

9. Robert Blauner, <u>Racial Oppression in America</u> (New York: Harper and Row,
    Publishers, 1972) pp. 18-45.

10. Fanon, op. cit., pp. 152-153.

11. Jean-Paul Sartre, <u>Orphee Noir</u>, preface to <u>Anthologie de la Nouvelle foesie
    Negre et Malgache</u> (Paris: Presses Universitaires de France, 1948, pp. XIff)
    in Frantz Fanon, <u>Black Skin, White Masks</u> (New York: Grove Press, Inc., 1967)
    pp. 132-133.

12. Fanon, <u>Wretched of the Earth</u>, op. cit., pp. 208-209.

13. Harold Cruse, <u>Rebellion or Revolution</u> (New York: William Marrow and Company,
    Inc., 1968) p. 66.

14. Ibid., p. 48.

15. Ibid., p. 15.

16. Ibid., p. 63.

17. Lerons Bennett, Jr., Ebony Magazine, August 1972, p. 33.

18. Ibid., p. 34.

19. Stokely Carmichael and Charles Hamilton, <u>Black Power</u> (New York: Vintage Books,
    1967) p. 53.

20. Sidney M. Willhelm, <u>Who Needs the Negro?</u> (New York: Anchor Books, 1971) p. 3.

21. Sidney M. Wilhelm, <u>Who Needs the Negro?</u> (New York: Anchor Books, 1971) p. 3.

22. Martin Kilson, Political Change in a West African State (Cambridge: Harvard University Press, 1971) p. 24.

23. Carmichael and Hamilton, op. cit., p. 4.

24. Charles E. Silberman, Crisis in Black and White (New York: Random House, 1968) p. 33.

25. Joel Kovel, White Racism: A Psycho-History (New York: Vintage Books, 1970) p. 3.

26. Carmichael and Hamilton, op. cit., p. 47.

27. Wilhelm, op. cit., pp. 1-2.

28. Ibid., p. 2.

29. Blauner, op. cit., p. 22.

30. Willhelm, op. cit., p. IX.

31. Ibid., p. 30.

32. Carmichael and Hamilton, op. cit., p. 32.

33. Robert Blauner, Racial Oppression in America (New York: Harper and Row, Publishers, 1972) pp. 19-49.

34. Immanuel Wallerstein, Africa, The Politics of Independence (New York: Vintage Books, 1961) p. 29.

35. Robert Blauner, Internal Colonialism and Ghetto Revolt, Social Problems, Vol. 16, No. 4, Spring 1969, p. 393.

36. Ibid., p. 395.

37. The American College Dictionary (New York: Random House, Publishers, 1967).

38. Blauner, op. cit., p. 395.

39. See Stanley Elkins, Slavery (Chicago: University of Chicago Press, 1969) pp. 81-140 and Frank Tannenbaum, Slave and Citizen (New York: Random House, 1946) for a discussion of the psychological aspects of slavery.

40. Blauner, op. cit., p. 395.

41. Wallerstein, op. cit., pp. 65-66.

42. Aristide R. Zolberg, One-Party Government in the Ivory Coast (Princeton: Princeton University Press, 1960) pp. 22-23.

43. James S. Coleman, The Politics of Sub-Saharan Africa, in Gabriel A. Almond and James S. Coleman, The Politics of Developing Areas (Princeton: Princeton University Press, 1960) p. 281.

44. Wallerstein, op. cit., p. 31.

45. Elkins, op. cit., p. 112.

46. The New York Times, February 15, 1974, p. 1.

47. Martin Kilson, <u>Political Change in a West African State</u> (Cambridge: Harvard University Press, 1966) p. 61.

48. Fanon, op. cit., p. 60.

Chapter 3

THE INTERNAL MODERNIZATION OF AFRO-AMERICANS

Oakland, California as demonstrated in Chapter 1, received its largest migration of black Americans during the period 1930 to 1970. Some of these migrants
being Southern agrarian lacked many of the skills necessary to make them productive
in a large Western urban environment. The efforts to equip and train the unskilled
has been a continuous process and has met with varying degrees of success.

The black bourgeoisie played a significant role in the psychological and intellectual preparation of the masses for urban living. The writing of the Honorable
J. C. Napier in the Oakland Sunshine in 1913 is indicative of the approach of the
bourgeoisie to this problem.

"All of life, rightly lived is simply a performance of duty, a passing
from one service to another, a sort of fermentation, as it were of one's
being.

If with the heritage received from his parentage, Frederick Douglass could
become the colossal figure which his memory presents in American history;
if John Mercer Langston , the only one of his race in the State of Virginia
to do so, could overcome the treachery of his own political household and
make his way from the plantation to the halls of congress; if Blanche K.
Bruce could make his way to the United States Senate; if Booker T. Washington
like the lowly Nazarene, born in obscurity, could by his own efforts and
undaunted courage, organize and equip one of the largest and most useful
schools in the land ... What I ask in all seriousness; with the advantages
which our schools afford our young men are their possibilities in the future?
They are simply unbounded and indescribable. They await well directed efforts
to raise themselves and their race to a level with all other people of this
great country. Will they respond to the gifts of nature and do their part
or will they sit and sing the song of the pessimist."[1]

In other cases the socialization of blacks to modern society began before their
arrival in the Oakland-San Francisco Bay area. Many were confronted with the need
for new skills after the American Civil War as a means of survival in the South.
Their change from a rural to an urban environment as a result of the population dislocation created by the War led to intensification of the internal modernization
process. Additional skills were necessary to compete successfully in an industrial
community. The changes required included organizational and institutional arrangements that were consistent with a process of internal secularization.

Seculari-ation is defined by Cino Germani as follows:

"Secularization is conceived here as a complex process including three basic
modifications of the social structures as follows: 1) Type of social action;
from prescriptive to elective action; 2) Acceptance of change from institutionalization of tradition to constitutionalization of change; 3) Institutional specialization from a relatively undifferentiated complex of
institutions ... These changes occur at different levels. At the psychological level, they affect attitudes and behavior, while at the normative
level, they affect institutions, values, statutes, roles and other norms.
They do not necessarily involve all the members of a society nor all types

of areas of behavior and attitudes, nor all institutions and values, secularization usually begins in relatively small groups, while the great majority of the population remains relatively unchanged. As for example involving either the transformation of pre-existing group attitudes is an expression of modification produced within the society. They constitute a reaction to the fact that certain institutions of the pre-existent social system no longer function as normatively expected. I am referring here to the active response or mobilization of the groups which are available by virtue of their disintegration and which in turn can generate innovations in both attitude and behavior. In a broad sense, to distinguish them from the masses, for even when the process of dislocation has affected large parts of the population, the active response begins to arise from small sectors, either because the impact is particularly great or because there are pre-existent elites or because new elites emerge from the interior of those sectors which are made 'available.' The active response, the so-called mobilization, of large segments of the population, also constitutes an essential aspect of modernization. But this aspect is a secondary process, that is a process that does not necessarily precede the first stages of the transition."[2]

Internal modernization is the process whereby people are prepared both individually and collectively and organizationally to play an effective role in modern society. If an internal colonization process is a valid concept as relates to the black man's position in American society, then it is highly consistent to posit a modernization process. This modernization process would necessarily by an internal modernizing process, primarily because it takes place within the broader context of the entire American society. It might explain the dynamics whereby a minority, colonized group that originated in a pre-industrial society developed a functional role and found a niche in the ongoing process of modernization of the larger community. This concept explains the adaptive changes of a colonized minority group in the political, social and economic areas that are necessary to bring about the desired degree of modernization and control over its own destinies. The primary differences in American internal modernization and the African modernization must fit into the mold of an existing modern system, and many of the decisions essential to this process are made by outsiders who have the ultimate power.

When placed in the context of the colonial analogy, internal modernization benefits both the colonizer and the colonized. It improves the opportunities for the oppressed to have some control over their socio-economic environment and it provides a ready pool of trained and productive labor to be exploited by the colonizer. The roles of the black bourgeoisie in these cases tends to be integrationist in the sense they are training members of the colonized class for roles in the colonizer's economic structure. On the other hand, they are often pressed by the colonized masses to retain the cultural identity of the oppressed. This produces a dilemma for the black middle class in defining its role in the system of race relations. The class becomes comparable to the classical colonial bourgeoisie. It becomes difficult to assess the overall significance of a person or movement for achievement of black aspirations in the society because blacks are disadvantaged not only by being oppressed, but also by not acquiring a level of modernization equal to the larger society as a historical result of that oppression. The black bourgeoisie may focus on rectification of economic disparities between whites and blacks. This action necessarily requires cooperation with white Americans and runs the risk of being misinterpreted by the masses who may perceive this cooperation as collaboration with the oppressors. In these instances the bourgeoisie loses effectiveness as an agent of modernization.

The roles of the black bourgeoisie in this modernization process are crucial to the existence in Oakland, California of either a viable community of Afro-Americans who are relatively self-sustaining or to the orderly integration of blacks into the m ainstream of the community. The black elite feel it has an obligation to lead the masses to modernization as indicated by the following responses:

Table 8

OBLIGATION TO COMMUNITY

Reply to: "Do you have obligations to the black community?"

	Traditional Elites (percent)	New Urban Elites (percent)
Have obligations	71	85
Do not have obligations	29	3
No response	0	12
Total	100	100

When they were asked to state their obligations , the following comments are typical of the responses:

"Being able to help them."
                              -Owner of body and fender shop

"Inform the community of the things to be done."
                              -Insurance salesman

"To have meetings , find out problems, set goals."
                              -Real Estate Agent

"Obligations to teach the youth and impress them with the needs of progress. I have an obligation to tell them the truth and not become a leader of the youth. Let them run to the show. I have an obligation to give back to the community some of the things they gave to me."
                              -Executive Administrator

"As an attorney, I have an obligation to serve them. I have an obligation to teach and open doors for them with the special skills they have."
                              -Attorney

"To educate and to provide inspiration."
                              -University Professor

"Helping them to get along."
                              -Liquor store owner

"Getting together to have meetings on issues pertaining to the pressures on our community."
                              -Beauty shop owner

"Give them the greatest degree of protection I can. Inspire the youth with recommendations and talk to their groups."
                              -Attorney

It is important to distinguish between their obligations to the black community and to the community as a totality, i.e., it is desirable to determine whether the middle-class feels that black community interests are more important to them than their commitment to the dominant society.

Table 9

GENERAL OBLIGATIONS

Reply to: "Do you feel that your obligations to the black community supercedes obligations to the broader community.

	Traditional Elites (percent)	New Urban Elites (percent)
Supercedes obligations to broader community	51	74
Do not supercede obligations to broader community	17	15
No response	32	11
Total	100	100

The foregoing indicates the black middle-class in the city of Oakland has a deep sense of responsibility and commitment to the total black community. It is apparent they are committed to the development of their community and this commitment is not impaired by their relative affluence. Again it must be reiterated, Frazier's analysis may be accurate given the parameters of his study. It should be noted that in the West, there is no large black leisure class. Most of those who comprise the black middle-class in the West achieved their status through accomplishment. Rising from humble means, generally the black middle-class tended to remain loyal to their communities.

In the colonial context, Kilson defines the modernization process as:

"The term 'modernization' refers to that complex of changes resulting from the contact of Western technological, industrial societies with the largely pre-literate (primitive) and pre-industrial societies of tropical Africa. These changes entail new patterns of social stratification centered on an impersonal market economy rather than the subsistence economy indigenous to African societies. Moreover, political institutions norms, and power configurations come to extend far beyond the former family, clan, lineage and tribal structures.[3]

Colonialism is not an essential pre-requisite of modernization. However, colonialism is such a disruptive force, it facilitates modernization by destroying or subjugating the traditional cultural and social values, thereby permitting the modernizing elite to initiate the process of modernization with little interference from the traditional authorities. Kilson speaks of this intrusive force in the African social change, it is of little value to view colonialism merely as a dominating system but also something more than this; it was a revolutionary system of social change in the context of pre-literate or pre-industrial societies.[4]

60

The net effects of the early experiences of black Americans was to create a climate of social mobilization that was to enable black Americans to cope with their new environment, i.e., Post Civil War situation. Social mobilization of large segments of a society, as seen by Germani is an essential aspect but is not necessarily a prerequisite of modernization and on occasion occurs simultaneously with modernization. This concept has defined as "the process in which major clusters of old, economic and psychological commitments are eroded and broken and people become available for new patterns of socialization and behavior."[5] Neil J. Smelsor, speaking of this concept, indicates:

"... that some of the main indices are exposure to aspects of modern life through demonstration of machinery, buildings , consumers' goods , etc.; response to mass media; change of residence; urbanization; change from agricultural occupations; literacy; growth of per capita income, etc."[6]

In the Afro-American experience social mobilization and internal modernization simultaneously evolved and is reinforced by the constant contact of the colonized with a dominant modern structure. In this context, internal modernization is defined in adaptive terms as an internally colonized society's ability to confront, overcome and indeed prepare itself for new challenges by rearranging its social structure. Whether challenges originate from internal technological, economic or social dynamics, from external contact, from the impact of natural forces or from other sources , internally modernizing societies must be able to accommodate to the need for change. Modernism in the internal colonial situation is the complete integration of the colonized into the social, political, technological and economic orders of the dominate society while simultaneously maintaining the identity and integrity of the subordinate group. In modernism the relationships of dominate and subordinate groups are transformed into a partnership in which these distinctions are no longer relevant.[7]

With the removal of slaves from their native African social and political institutions, a period of social mobilization evolved in America, that made a modernization process inevitable. After the American Civil War, Afro-Americans began to modernize at a rapid pace spurred by the necessity of surviving in an industrial society. Social mobilization made the imposition of a modernization process relatively easy. It simply replaced most of the traditional systems and co-existed with any residue of those systems. There was little need to interact with African traditional systems in America because they were impotent and unable to compete with the modernizing forces.

Although several prominant scholars have engaged in debate regarding the effects of Western civilization on the traditional African culture of black slaves , there is consensus that the effects were significant if not devastating. E. Franklin Frazier, the noted black sociologist, has stated that on the plantation in the Southern states, the Negro slave shed off most completely his African heritage. The African family system was destroyed and the slave was separated from his kinsmen and friends. Indeed the slave was not permitted even in chance encounter with friends to converse in his native language. However, there are others, perhaps the most prominant among them is Melville J. Herskovits who maintains that under one of the most inhumane slave systems ever devised by mankind there were many examples of cultural survival that were retained by the slaves and incorporated into their survival mechanisms.

Regardless of the merit of the arguments presented by Frazier and Herskovits, we can logically infer that the impact of the institution of slavery on the cultural and psychological well-being of slaves was significant. It can also be inferred and substantiated that cultural and psychological dominance was a means whereby a foreign people were kept under control and owned as chattel. It is sufficient for our discussion to note that the nature of this dominance was such that it facilitated social mobilization and modernization of a people without regard for cultural restraints. Indeed it was absolutely necessary to proceed with some degree of modernization in order to make the slave a viable unit within the plantation economy.

The task of modernizing slaves was rendered less difficult in the American colonies than in Brazil and other South American countries in view of the type of African brought here. Eugene D. Genovese makes the point that:

"It has long been falsely assumed that since slave traders mixed their cargoes, all parts of the hemisphere received similarly mixed bags. But Brazil, for example, declined large numbers of Angolans and Congolese, whose military, religious and cultural traditions made them especially difficult to control. Brazil also received a large number of Muslim slaves from Upper Guinea who proved intractable everywhere in the hemisphere. The United States, on the other hand largely drew its slaves from those portions of Lower Guinea which had a population previously disciplined to servitude and dominations. Ironically, these Africans were in some respect, among the most advanced in technical culture."[8]

It seems to be characteristic of a defeated people to move to attain the level of technology of the conquerors. This is true whether the defeated nation remains intact or whether they are dispersed as was the case of European plundering of the African peoples. In many instances they will discard the traditions and technology that seemed previously appropriate for the advanced technology of the conquerors. This phenomenon was observed by Stanley Elkins in his study of the Jewish people in German concentration camps in World War II. If Genovese's argument concerning the characteristics of Africans prior to European slavery is correct, it can be readily seen why American blacks were conducive to slavery and the modernization process.[9]

Stanley M. Elkins, Joseph A. Tillinghast and E. Franklin Frazier among others present a different portrait of the African slave. Elkins makes the point that as the continent of Africa was vast, Africans were brought to European traders from many different places. The trading stations were scattered over large areas of the West Coast of Africa and it was usual for slaves to be brought from great distances inland. The slaves had a variety of religious customs, social and political arrangements and languages. He further indicates that actually it was the very distances between tribes, the hopeless diversity of languages, and the Negroes' inability to communicate with one another, that was counted on to minimize the danger of insurrections on shipboard.[10]

Elkins and Genovese agree that servitude and domination existed in Africa prior to the European incursions. However, Elkins does not consider this fact as relevant when evaluating the personality of the African slave in America. Elkins asserts that there was a sharp distinction between the domestic slavery prevalent among the tribes themselves and the state into which the departed captives ultimately were to be delivered by the Europeans. There was little in the one experience that could prepare a man for what he would experience in the other.[11]

In developing his portrait of the African captured by Europeans and transported to America. Elkins and Genovese found that there was indeed an African technology on the mainland prior to the European experience. Elkins further found that there was a closely knit family structure, political, economic and legal institutions. There was a rule of law, a traditional constitution tax and revenue structure, military system and an intricate system of inferior and superior courts. The typical West African tribesman was warlike, had a profound sense of family authority, and took hard work for granted. He was accustomed to living by a highly formalized set of rules.[12]

In reviewing the historical data pertaining to the culture of Africans prior to their captivity and the many learned conclusions of scholars on the subject, Elkins clearly concludes that there is little in these studies to explain the impact of slavery on the personality of the black slaves. The change effected by the impact of slavery was to lead to rapid social mobilization and modernization in the European dominated Americas. The behavior of blacks in slavery and their adaptability to the modernization process are readily explainable when their cultural experiences are understood.

The social-psychological impact of slavery on the African people, as practiced in America, was highly conducive to the instigation of the modernization process. John Hope Franklin believes that slavery in the Spanish colonies was less harsh than slavery in the English colonies. In the Spanish colonies there was severity in many laws, cruelty on the part of many slaveholders, but the influence of the Catholic Church mitigated the harshness of the institution. Another reason for the difference in degrees of cruelty was the dispersal of slaves over a larger area and the willingness of Spaniards to intermarry with blacks on a respectable basis. These variables suggested by Franklin not only mitigated the harshness of slavery, but prevented the rapid modernization of the Spanish colonies and their slaves. They removed the necessity of black modernization for survival as was the case in the English colonies.[13]

Elkins agrees with Franklin on the relative harshness of slavery in North America and South America. However, there is a very little agreement on the effects of slavery on the personalities of the slaves and the slaves ability to adapt to a new situation where survival was dependent on his ability to find a niche in an ongoing new social situation. Elkins' argument is that American slavery was a closed institution, and as such, produced a "Sambo" type personality. He infers that this demeanor was the general personality type among slaves on antebellum plantations and in many ways were comparable to the situations of Jews incarcerated in concentration camps by the Germans in World War II.

An evaluation of the two situations, slavery and German concentration camps, may reveal some similar situations, but available evidence does not indicate the blacks, who were enslaved, perceived their situation as being hopeless or a closed system. This assertion is supported by the repeated attempts of many to escape, the knowledge of freedmen and the limited use of manumission usually upon the death of a master. So in the case of the blacks there was an element of hope. On the other hand, the genecide perpetrated on the heroic Jewish people by Germany left little hope for these incarcerated. The system was totally closed and it is possible that the Jewish prisoners perceived their situation as being closed.[14]

A brief discussion of the psychological dynamics involved in the above situation is germane to the thesis of modernization in an internal colonial situation, because it demonstrates the social psychological climate of the black people when initially placed in a modernizing environment. Elkins reveals the shock most blacks must have felt at being captured in battle, and a second great shock when they made the long march to the sea under glaring sun from their native homes inland. He also mentions the shock of the middle passage and being sold to European slavers. Similarly in the situation of the Jews, he believes their arrests were engineered to produce the maximum terrorist effect, a shock. Often these arrests occurred in the middle of the night and the prisoner was abruptly taken from his familiar environment and thrust into an alien system.

He indicates that the SS Guards were similar to the slavers, because the prisoners were dehumanized until they were simple children, looking to the guards as the father image. The guards were the bearers of all good things, food, clothing and other necessities; therefore, the Jews tried to please them and became more like them. The result of the treatment by the guards was reflected in a complete breakdown of all standards and norms of the prisoner group. Elkins says that the fact that the rules were strict, the guards having life and death power and the prospect of a limitless future in confinement led to a psychic displacement.[15]

The trauma of one being wrenched suddenly from one social mileau and placed in another was the experience of both the black slaves and the Jewish people of Germany. The failure of native institutions to protect them when protection was most needed undoubtedly had some effect on prevalent norms and values. There was an immediate need to establish new relationships and institutions to cope with their new situations. There was also a very real need to survive until such time as means to control their situations were developed. However, there was a difference in the two situations that should not be ignored. In the case of the European Jews there was an attempt to totally exterminate them; however, in the black slave case, there was an attempt to totally eradicate their previous existence as an organized people and to make them into a useful colonial commodity. Although the effects were similar in many ways this distinction is useful in analyzing the interaction of blacks in an internal colonial situation.

Certainly, to the unsophisticated observer, the groping by both groups to find new meaning and new definitions in their situations would appear as immature or childlike. Indeed the dehumanizing process they went through left them with few alternatives other than to rely on their often sadistic respective masters for creature needs. These proud people were reduced to the level of having to be completely resocialized because they were not prepared for these new experiences.

The Early Period of Social Mobilization and Internal Modernization of Blacks in America

Essential to internal modernization is a modernizing intellectual elite, a vanguard. C. E. Black indicates that importance of intellectuals in the modernization process:

"It is appropriate to start with the intellectual realm, since the growth of man's understanding and control over his environment in all of its complexity plays such a vital role in the process of change in modern times. Indeed, it is clear that in a sense little has changed except man's knowledge, for the diversity of the physical environment was present before man began to understand its potentialities, and evolutionary changes in man and his environment have not been significant in historical times."[16]

Among the early black modernizing elites we find the following who published narratives or newspapers in an effort to produce a modernizing psychological climate among blacks and whites in the United States between 1840 and 1860; William Wells Brown, Lunsford Lane, Moses Grandy, Frederick Douglass, Lewis Clarke, Julius Melbourne, Henry Bibb, J. W. C. Pennington, Solomon Northrup, Austin Steward, N. W. Loguen, William C. Niel, Martin E. Delaney and James McCune Smith. Because of their subjects, most of these narratives had a dramatic quality that the imagination along would have difficulty achieving, however there is no reason to believe that all of the hairraising episodes occurred just as they were told.[17]

The black newspapers were to play an important role in this internal modernizing process. Among the best known of the first black newspapers were Freedom's Journal, started by Samuel Cornish and John Russwurn in 1827 and the North Star, started in 1847 and later was changed to Frederick Douglass' Paper in 1850. This paper was published by Frederick Douglass and enjoyed wide circulation for several years. Other early, short-lived papers included, The Mystery (Pittsburg, 1843); The Colored Man's Journal (New York, 1851); The Mirror of the Times (San Francisco, 1855); and The Anglo-African (New York, 1859).[18]

The importance of black journalism upon the internal modernization process cannot be over-emphasized. It was largely through the efforts of the black intellectuals, who published these journals and newspapers that the black American masses came into contact with the industrialization and urbanization processes in the early Twentieth century. Franklin gives us an illustration of the part they played:

"... The severe labor depression in the South in 1914 and 1915 sent wages down to 75 cents per day and less. The damage of the boll weevil to cotton crops in 1915 and 1916 discouraged many. Floods in the summer of 1915 left thousands of Negroes destitute and homeless and ready to accept almost anything in preference to the uncertainty of life in the South. Meanwhile, the wheels of Northern industry were turning more rapidly than ever, and the demand for laborers was increasing. The sharp decline in foreign immigration from more than one million in 1914 to slightly more than three hundred thousand in the following year, created a labor shortage that sent agents scurrying to the South to entice Negroes as well as whites to move North to secure employment in industry. Injustice in the Southern courts, lack of privileges, disfranchisement, segregation, and lynching several as important stimuli for Negroes to move out of the South. The North came to be regarded as the 'land of promise' and the Negro press did much to persuade Southern Negroes to abandon the existence which held nothing better for them than second-class citizenship. The Chicago Defender exclaimed, 'To die from the bite of frost is far more glorious than at the hands of a mob.' In 1917, The Christian Recorder wrote, 'If a million Negroes move north and west in the next twelve months, it will be one of the greatest things for the Negro since the Emancipation Proclamation.' In 1916, the movement spread like wild fire among Negroes ... By summer of that year the migration had reached flood-tide in the states of the deep South."[19]

Basically, modernizing black leaders have split in the debate regarding the best method to achieve modernization along two lines of action. One is essentially an assimilationist position, the other a separatist. This debate has raged from the times of Frederick Douglass, integrationist, and Martin Delany, separationist, to the present times when the debate was continued by Malcolm X, Elijah Muhammad, separationists, and Martin Luther King and Roy Wilkins, integrationists. There has been little change in the relative positions of these points of view over the years. In spite of this dialogue, or maybe because of it, modernization has proceeded in nearly all sectors of political, social and economic life of black Americans.

Early progress in the field of education is reported by Franklin as follows:

"The results of the efforts to insure the education of Negroes were gratifying. In 1900 there were 28,560 Negro teachers. At the same time there were more than 1,500,000 Negro children in schools, thirty-four institutions for Negroes were reported as giving collegiate training, and a large number of Negroes were being permitted to enter the universities and colleges of the North ... By 1900 more than 2,000 Negroes had graduated from institutions of higher learning, while more than 700 were in colleges at that time.[20]

Modernization of the educational institutions was to continue until the historic Supreme Court decision in Brown vs. Board of Education in 1954, requiring all the public schools in the country to integrate. This ruling freed black leaders to change their focus from the opportunity for education to the quality of education. The modernization of educational institutions for black Americans is a clear vivid illustration of the internal process at work. It is obvious that blacks did not have the means of power to force this decision upon the nation but through adept manipulation of the judicial and political processes, and with the help of white leaders, their efforts culminated in a partial victory.

This internal modernizing process has continued from generation to generation principally among elites. There has been considerable effort to develop and co-ordinate the elites expertise and to elevate and assist others in finding a niche in modernization. There was very little accomplished in terms of modernization of Afro-Americans prior to the Nineteenth century. The Seventeenth and Eighteenth centuries were eras that focused more on social mobilization than modernization although both processes were discernible in this period. In the various regions of the country social mobilization and modernization preceded simultaneously and at differentiated speeds dictated by the social and economic realities of the area.

Among the early giants in internal modernization we find Booker T. Washington. Washington was one of the founders of Tuskegee Institute in 1881. In 1900 he founded the National Negro Business League and in five years it grew to more than 100 chapters. Franklin says:

"Washington never tired of urging Negroes to develop habits and skills that would win for them places in their Southern communities ... He said that he believed that for years to come the education of the people of my race should be so directed that the greatest proportion of the mental strength of the masses will be brought to bear upon the everyday practical things of life, upon something that is needed to be done and something which they will be permitted to do in the community in which they reside."[21]

Under the leadership of Washington, Tuskegee Institute developed into one of the leading industrial and technological institutions for black students of higher education in the United States. The graduates of this institution were extremely useful when America mobilized in World War II to meet the threat of foreign aggression.

One of Washington's leading critics and himself a giant in the modernization of black America was W. E. B. Dubois. In his Souls of Black Folk, he wrote several critical essays on Washington's policies. He did not approve of the way Washington ignored the white South's reduction of the black's political and civil status. Further, although he appreciated the need for black skilled craftsmen, he was more interested in the intellectual fulfillment of the black scholar. In any case, both of these titans were to have their way to a degree as black Americans progressed both in the trades and intellectual pursuits.[22]

During the period of National Reconstruction, blacks began to establish labor organizations to represent the workers' interest and to improve the living conditions of Afro-Americans. In 1869 Isaac Myers founded the National Colored Labor Union. Blacks had been refused entry into the established white labor organizations. At the first convention there were over two hundred delegates. This union proved to be too weak to bargain effectively with employers.[23]

In the same year, The Knights of Labor was founded as a secret labor union open to all races. With the help of black organizers, their black membership soon grew to sixty thousand. Southern states drove the organizers out of the South.

In 1900, only thirty-two thousand blacks were in labor unions. The United Mine Workers had twenty thousand Afro-American members. Approximately one thousand were union carpenters. The balance were in other organized labor unions. Afro-Americans were systematically excluded from the American Federation of Labor that accepted only skilled laborers. Blacks were rarely admitted to this union.[24]

Perhaps the next most important black in the field of modernization in the economic area is A. Phillip Randolph, who organized the pullman porters' union in August 1925 and was chiefly responsible for organizing the First March on Washington in June 1941. This organization led to the famous Presidential Executive Order 8802, dated June 25, 1941, prohibiting discrimination in employment in defense industries and in the government. Organizing in the field of labor continues under different leaders but again this is a clear indication of the effectiveness of the internal modernization process when it is manipulated by intelligent leaders.[25]

Legal as well as other institutions are transformed in the modernization process. In the Nineteenth Century, Chief Justice Tanney's ruling in Dred Scott v. Sanford that Scott could not sue because he was not a citizen of the United States, seriously impeded the progress of a modernizing society, and more specifically, impeded the progress of the black minorities colonized in America. Although the blacks were in a modernizing environment, their efforts to be included in the modernizing process would be seriously damaged by this ruling. Indeed, this ruling would keep them tied to the traditional forces in America, mostly in the Southern part of the country, and in competition with the forces of industrialization in the North. In the context of modernization, whereby traditional colonial institutions are transformed, it is the process that transforms both institutions and is part of an adaptive process that occurs during modernization.[26]

Tanney's ruling would effectively deny blacks the mobility that is essential to a modernizing people. His decision was met with resistance by some of the prominent politicians of this time in American History. The initiative to bring blacks into the process was taken up by the Congress. In April 1862, Congress abolished slavery in the District of Columbia. The Confiscation Act of July 1862, provided that all slaves of persons engaged in rebellion or in any way giving aid thereto, who should be captured or escape to Union lines shall be deemed captives of war, and shall be forever free of their servitude and not again held as slaves. This action was promptly followed by President Lincoln's Emancipation Proclamation on January 1, 1863. The Thirteenth Amendment to the Constitution, abolishing slavery, was proclaimed on December 18, 1865, ending the question of involuntary servitude in the country, but it did not help to raise the blacks to a level of equality in regards to citizenship.[27]

The modernization of bureaucracies and institutions is strongly resisted by traditional forces in a colonizing situation. Some modernization of the structures of the colonizer's society is necessary if an internally colonized people are to be functional in the social and economic structures. The traditional forces in America were quick to react to the actions of the Congress and President by implementing the so-called "Black Codes" in 1865 and 1866. These codes were similar to ante-bellum slave codes. They carried severe penalties for vagrancy and lent support to the establishment of black peonage. They were designed to impose and retain an inferior status on blacks.[28]

Having resolved the question of involuntary servitude, the Congress moved to remedy the confusion brought about by the Dred Scott decision as regards citizenship for blacks. The Fourteenth Amendment to the Constitution was adopted. It provided in its first sentence that "All persons born or naturalized in the United States, and subject to the jurisdiction thereof, are citizens of the United States, and of the State wherein they reside."[29] This Amendment was proclaimed on March 30, 1870.

Two years later on March 30, 1872, the Fifteenth Amendment to the Constitution was ratified. It proclaimed that "The right of citizens of the United States to vote shall not be denied or abridged by the United States or by any State on account of race, color or previous condition of servitude ..."[30] Although blacks were already modernizing at a rapid rate, this chain of events in the country was to give this modernizing process impetus without destroying the nature of the colonial relationship.

The following agencies were to play a major role in the early modernization of the American blacks: The Army utilized black soldiers introducing them to modern warfare; black schools, the Bureau of Refugees, Freedom and Abandoned Land (The Freedmen's Bureau) and the Black Churches. In an internal colonial situation, the modernization of the colonized group can only be accomplished through the combined efforts of the colonizer and the colonized. Modernization cannot be realized for the subordinate group unless the colonizers perceive that it is in their own best interest. The colonizer usually dictates the spheres of social activity to be modernized such as political, economic, educational and others, and the methods the colonized may use to proceed with modernization is also indicated by the colonizer. In this way internal colonization does not differ significantly from classical colonization. However, internal modernization differs greatly with the modernization of emerging nations. In the latter situation, modernization proceeds in an international atmosphere of competition and inter-dependence based upon the emerging nations' perceptions of their needs and the flexibility of their political and cultural institutions.

In terms of internal modernization of American blacks, the successful conclusion of the Civil War by the modernizing forces of the North was decisive. At the end of this war, blacks were torn from the traditional institution of slavery and forced into a situation where modernization was necessary for their survival. In spite of this situation, it is doubtful that any meaningful effort to industrialize blacks would have taken place if it was not considered in the best interest of the dominant racial group.

Partly for humanitarian reasons and the necessity of stabilizing a fluid social situation, the Congress of the United States established the Freedmen's Bureau. This Bureau relieved much suffering for the blacks who were recently emancipated. In less than two years there were forty-six hospitals under the Bureau staffed with physicians, surgeons and nurses. The death rate among blacks was reduced and sanitary conditions improved.[31]

The Freedmen's Bureau resettled 30,000 persons because of an urgent need for labor and the Bureau distributed some land to freedmen. Colonies of infirm, destitute and vagrant blacks were set up in several states. The Bureau supervised and aided blacks in finding employment and securing appropriate wages for their labor. It organized freedmen's courts and boards of arbitration. It set up or supervised schools of all kinds: day, night, Sunday and industrial schools, as well as colleges. Several of the black colleges of this period received support from this Bureau. They include Howard University, Hampton Institute, St. Augustine's College, Atlanta University, Fisk University, Storer College and Johnson C. Smith University.[32]

In addition to the efforts of the United States Congress to make black Americans viable and productive in an internal colonial situation, some religious institutions were operative in the process. For instance, the American Missionary Association, the Baptists, Methodists, Presbyterians and Episcopalians established schools. By 1870, there were 247,333 pupils in 4,329 schools.[33] John H. Franklin, speaking of the education of blacks during this period says, "The shortcomings in their education arose not from a want of zeal on the part of teachers, but from ignorance of the needs of Negroes and from the necessary preoccupation of students with the problem of survival in a hostile world ..."[34]

In classical colonial societies the vehicle for mobilizing the masses for education in the industrialization and modernization concepts is usually the mass party system. The nature of the internal colonial relationship between the colonizer and the colonized and the close demographic proximity of the two groups does not lend itself to this solution to the problems of mobilization. In America, during the early stages of internal modernization, the black American church fulfilled this function within the framework permissible by the realities of internal colonization.

Shortly after the Civil War, the membership in older black churches rose greatly. For instance, the African Methodist Episcopal Church which had only 20,000 members in 1856, boasted 75,000 ten years later; in 1876 its membership exceeded 200,000. Other congregations were formed. Many of those new congregations were established by blacks who defected from established white organizations.[35]

These churches' roles in the modernization process can not be over emphasized. In the first place, in view of the social disruption created by the war, in many instances, they substituted for the extended family that some blacks had been accustomed to in the rural, pre-war environment. The provided material and psychological support to those who were pressing for better opportunities for oppressed blacks within the limits of internal colonialism. Therefore, they provided a means whereby blacks could pool their resources to advance themselves economically and help others who were less fortunate. Lastly, it furnished the newly enfranchised blacks with a value system and creed, the Protestant Ethic, that was conducive to rapid modernization.

Banks were established to encourage blacks to save their money. Among these were the Free Labor Bank at New Orleans; The Freedman Savings and Trust Company established by the Federal government and the Freedman's Bank in 1865 that grew to 34 branches by 1872. Frederick Douglass was made president of the Freedman's Bank in 1874. In addition to these banks and consistent with the Protestant Ethic and capitalism in 1865, blacks of Baltimore organized the Chesapeake and Marine Railway and Dry Dock Company and many smaller private firms.[36]

Black churches and the Protestant Ethic served the colonized blacks well in the early stages of modernization. However, there are strong indications that both have been dysfunctional to blacks in achieving their objectives in the second half of the Twentieth Century. In many places in the colonized community, this Western European value system is being replaced by a concept of black culture that has not been defined. It has not been defined in the sense that there is no generally acceptable value system activated by the proponents of this concept. The true test of this new concept will be whether it is conducive to the modernization process and if it continues to provide for the rapid modernization of blacks in a colonial situation.

It seems that there must be a change of the value systems of the colonizer and the colonized if blacks are to achieve their maximum level of modernity. Whereas, the Protestant Ethic was immensely valuable in the early stages it does not lend itself to modernization of Afro-Americans in a subordinate position in a modern society. This is the task of black culture and this is the problem that must be resolved if the concept of blackness is a viable one. A value system must be created to cope with modernization and to influence human behavior by establishing guidelines for interpersonal relationships and moral behavior.

The New Internal Modernizing Elite

There are several major social, political and economic groups within the classical concept of colonialism. Among them are the colonializing power, the traditional elites, the intelligentsia or new elites and the masses. In the African situation the colonial powers were Western European nations. The traditional elites are tribal chiefs and religious leaders. The intelligentsia or new elitists are composed of the Western educated professionals who exert a significant degree of power over the urban masses.

In the context of internal colonialism is America, the traditional elites were those who rose to prominence in the black community after the initial destruction of African culture. They quickly assimilated the values of Western European culture and the Protestant ethic and emulated the white society. Although their economic base and source of legitimacy was primarily in the black community, with a further degree of legitimacy accorded by the colonizer in that they were recognized as intermediaries, they resented the ignorance of lower class blacks and their life styles. The resentment, notwithstanding, they often tried to improve the conditions of the colonized generally.

Their role in the colonial situation is crucial because they perceive themselves as being the leaders of the oppressed minority and their spokesman. It is largely through this group that modernization of the masses took place and prior to 1963 it was through this group that benefits for the masses were channeled. They determined the priorities of modernization and social action. They determined what was considered proper or respectable behavior for the masses, rewarding correct behavior and demeanor by controlling social mobility.

They performed a very essential function and were ligitimized by both the colonizers and the colonized. It is partly through their efforts in socializing the masses to a degree of acceptance of their situation and their adherence to Western European culture that assists the colonizer in terms of social control. Physical barricades, such as police and standing armies, are seldom necessary to divide the colonizer's property from that of the colonized and agitation for revolutionary changes are kept within the framework of the colonizer's tolerance limits. Although the demographic location of blacks and other minorities of color in America is very similar to those of a classical colonial situation and these oppressed groups number tens of millions of persons, they are usually effectively controlled with a relatively minor display of police power. This is not to imply that the colonizer's police are not visable, because they certainly are deployed throughout the community of the colonized but their numbers are small in relation to the size and physical power of the oppressed minorities.

One of the instruments of the middle class' power in the black community is their ability to influence the actions of the masses. The bourgeoisie was queried on this point:

Table 10

INFLUENCE OF BLACK SPOKESMEN

Reply to: "Do you feel that certain blacks influence opinion and actions of other blacks in this community?"

	Traditional Elites (percent)	New Urban Elites (percent)
Blacks influence opinion	74	77
Blacks do not influence opinion	26	11
No response	0	12
Total	100	100

It was found, the middle class felt that many blacks had an effective voice in the formulation of black responses and shaping opinion in the community. These included elected officials, politicians, attorneys, physicians, community organizers, the upper echelons of the Black Panther Party, members of the Nation of Islam, governmental administrators and officials, ministers and others.

This group which is considered the upper class of the colonized, is often maligned by radical groups that feel they are an impediment to black liberation. Any objective study of the traditional elites will reveal that much of the leadership in civic action and many of the effective programs in the modernization of blacks prior to 1963 were brought about through the efforts of this class. In view of their adherence to conservative methods of internal modernization, they must be considered the traditional forces in the colonized community. In view of the dynamics of the process, the modernizing elite of the period of time often becomes the traditional elite of a more advanced period. Hence, organizations that are considered traditional protest groups in 1970, i.e., The National Urban League and the National Association for the Advancement of Colored People may well have been the new elites of the early and mid-twentieth century.

71

The black elites cannot be distinguished from the masses on the basis of occupation and income alone "for neither occupation nor income is, in the final
analysis, the decisive measuring rod. Rather, the middle-class is marked off from
the lower class by a pattern of behavior expressed in stable family and associational relationships ... All this finds an objective measure in standard of living--
the way people spend their money, and in public behavior."[37] The manner in which
they spend their money and public behavior are the means whereby the intermediaries
control and mobilize the masses in the internal modernization process. Since they
seemingly possess more material wealth than the masses their influence is enhanced
because of their appearance of having found a niche in the society that is far superior to the lower colonized classes.

In their study of black stratification in Chicago, St. Clair Drake and Horace R.
Cayton found that when blacks were asked to name upper-class individuals, a number
of prominent professionals were pointed out such as doctors, lawyers, newspaper
editors, politicians and political leaders. They noted that wealth alone was not
sufficient to qualify for this distinction. This upper-class was found to have
more than average education and perhaps more importantly were considered by the
masses to be leaders of the race. This upper-class role as intermediaries is brought
sharply into focus by this study. From the viewpoint of the colonizer, this group
could be trusted because of their acculturation to Western European values and their
relative conservatism. At the same time, they were perceived by lower-class blacks
as spokesmen, and representatives of their cause.[38]

This class of intermediaries was only moderately wealthy. Indeed, in many instances, based on the criterion of wealth, they would have ranked in the lower
middle-class of the dominant society. More fundamentally, their position as upper-
class in the colonized community is based on the perceptions of the lower classes
of their devotion and contributions to the race and to their desire to get ahead in
a rapidly modernizing environment. Most very large incomes usually resulted from
investments in real estate, Negro business or securities other than salaries and fees
received from their professions.[39]

Intermediaries were usually well-trained in both their professions and the problems of race relations. They were called upon by members of the dominant group to
articulate the needs of the oppressed and to administer programs designed to assist
them. This intermediary group recognizes each other as upper-class and considers
themselves as equals to each other in social status. They consider each other as
fit associates for social affairs, marriage partners and intimate friendships. As
the elders die off, middle-aged professional families assume their positions.[40]

One of the physical characteristics of this group is a high percentage of light-
skinned or near whites. The exclusiveness of their social clubs and apparent preference to associate with each other has produced cleavages in the oppressed community
based upon skin color. This is a natural consequence of the legacy of domination
and slavery. In view of some, it is a cleavage between house blacks and field hands.
Misorganization in colonial America, as has been manifest usually involved fornica-
tion between white men and black women, though the opposite combination was common
far more than is generally supposed. The dominance of white men in America over the
colonized blacks extended to the bed, where the sex act itself served as a ritualis-
tic reenactment of their daily pattern of social dominance. Slavery and inter interracial relationships were the bedrock facts which so powerfully influenced, perhaps even determined, the kind of society which emerged in America.[41]

Given the closeness of the interracial relationship in a colonized situation, it was inevitable that a significant percentage of the population would become both black and white or conversely neither black nor white. E. Franklin Frazier, in his study of the black bourgeoisie, found that this upper class group was without cultural roots in either the black world with which it refused to identify, or the white world which refused to permit the black bourgeoisie to share its life. However, the nature of their relationships to the dominant groups led to distinct advantages over their darker skinned brothers in concrete terms such as better education, higher standards of living and the ability to find a niche in the modernization process of the larger society.[42]

There is evidence and data to substantiate Frazier's point of view in regards to the frustration and self-seeking of a significant percentage of this intermediary group. Any objective analysis of their behavior will have to concede that the internal modernization of blacks in America would have been greatly impeded without their expertise in organization and advocacy for a better life for the oppressed lower classes and their leadership in providing a framework of action that has led to the few benefits the black community enjoys in their colonized position in America.

After their perception of rejection by the dominant group to assimilation, especially after achieving recognition in their various professional fields, this upper-class turned in their frustration to ardent race and civil rights advocacy. Their role in the internal modernization of blacks has a prominent positive position in the history of the Afro-American experience. After the Civil War, many white teachers staffed the educational institutions of the former slaves, but as the number of black teachers grew, they gradually took over some of the schools with the result that in many communities of the South, the education and socialization of blacks were largely in the hands of this upper-class. Although they articulated many of the values of the dominate community, these intermediaries placed a strong emphasis on racial pride, excellence and achievement. It was largely through their efforts that succeeding generations of blacks have been able to generally cope with the ongoing process of modernization.

In other professions such as law, medicine and business, often at their personal expense, this group trained, educated, organized and fought for the betterment of the oppressed. Few have suffered the indignities of personal danger that those of the legal profession have endured in their championship of unpopular causes and clients on behalf of the black oppressed people. Doctors by virtue of the colonized situation of their race have devoted time, energy and other personal resources to fight disease and illness in areas where white doctors have exhibited very little interest. The ministers of the various denominations have strongly emphasized a value system and moral code of thrift, community concern and hard work that has served the colonized blacks well until recent times. In this connection, Frazier's characterization is only partially correct.

The foregoing, notwithstanding, the colonized bourgeoisie can properly be criticized for their exclusiveness. In spite of their actions on behalf of the black community in the field of civil rights and modernization, their tending to remove themselves socially from that community and to form cliques, led to distrust and animosity in the colonized community. In this class of intermediaries, both female and male clubs made a fetish of exclusiveness and in view of the skin color difference, reenforced the notion that blackness was inferior. This exclusiveness led to serious consequences for their leadership roles as their masses began to agitate for liberation from the oppressiveness of their white dominators. They suffered the wrath of larger lower classes for their failure to identify with the masses generally, and their class identification with the white colonizers.[43]

The characteristics of the black bourgeoisie as seen by the middle class respondents are: Conspicuous consumption, they have titles such as Doctor, Professor, Attorney; they alienate themselves from contact with the common black person; they have high income levels, residence and occupation; they are achievers; aloofness, better occupations articulate, educated leaders; different life styles and titles; disassociation with fellow brothers and sisters and more effective associations with the white middle class.

St. Clair Drake and Horace R. Cayton in their study of Chicago found that:

"Skin color is not an important factor in upper class male clubs although at least one male club has been accused of being blue-vein. According to upper-class gossip, this club came into being in the early twenties and has several very dark members. They felt they were not wanted and withdrew to form a rival club. A member of the older club, in giving his version of the split, did not deny that the original club was 'light.'"[44]

The problem of race and identity in a colonized situation has met with several responses by the colonized people. In some cases as the colonized attempt to improve their conditions and get ahead they will adopt the cultural values of the colonized to the extent they will deny their heritage and denigrate their own people and color. They tend to attribute virtue and goodness to whiteness and dirtiness and laziness to blackness.

Citizens of the middle-class in Oakland indicate that there were in the past a few organizations and clubs in the area that catered only to light-skinned blacks. A long time resident of the community expressed his anguish at being doubly discriminated against because his skin is dark. He indicated that while attending school or seeking employment he would be discriminated against in the white community and discriminated against socially in the black community. This particular individual is happy with the black power movement that gives dignity and respect to dark skinned blacks.

The black power movement, notwithstanding, there are members of the black middle class in Oakland who feel that skin color is important in achievement in America. One prominent administrator stated that as much as he detested the situation, any objective study would indicate the media and other employers seemingly prefer hiring light skinned blacks. Since people of the same socio-economic background usually prefer each others companionship, skin color is still important in determining who gets ahead in spite of recent movements to eliminate its importance. The following table addresses this question.

Table 11

SKIN COLOR

Reply to: "Is skin color important in aiding blacks to get ahead?"

	Traditional Elites (percent)	New Urban Elites (percent)
Skin color important	29	40
Skin color not important	37	23
No response	34	37
Total	100	100

The differences in the perceptions of the two elites on this question are significant. The traditionals are relatively secure in their position in the community and of course, if skin color is important within the community they would have to share some of the responsibility for its persistence. On the other hand, the new urban elites would most likely be victims of skin color discrimination as they gain affluence and seek to enter associations that rival the traditionals for prestige. Of crucial importance is the fact many of both groups feel there is a dual discrimination that inhibits the advancement of dark skinned blacks in Oakland. All respondents agree, the question of skin color is diminishing within the community and probably would not exist if it was not supported by selective employment on the part of the white community. As the black community becomes politically aware, these differences tend to decrease.

The exclusiveness of the black bourgeoisie is partly due to vested interest. The class interest has both psychological and economical commitments to the society of the colonizer. As members of a relatively elite group, they have exposure to the advanced educational systems of the colonizer and many are inducted into the value and normative systems of the colonizer. This action on their part is usually re-enforced by gains in material wealth that requires their participation in the economic system of the dominate culture. The same system that provides for their affluence, simultaneously oppresses the colonized as a class. This creates a dilemma for the middle-class blacks who realize the injustices of the system, but feel they have to support it to maintain their current status in the society as intermediaries and spokesmen for the colonized as a class. Their vested interest becomes a tool of social control.

In a sense, their exclusiveness alienated them from the masses for often in such basic matters as religious institutions this elite chose to lean toward denominations that were exclusive. For instance, Drake and Cayton inform us that their study revealed the upper classes and were usually affiliated with the Congregationalist, Episcopalians or Presbyterians. There were a few affiliated with the African Methodist Episcopal Church which is a relatively high status church in the black community. While these churches were not "blue vein" they do perhaps have a higher percentage of light members than other churches in the black community. They avoided membership in many Baptist and Holiness churches where the largest percentage of blacks congregated.[45]

In nearly all areas of social life the dichotomy between the intermediaries and the masses are evident. The upper-classes, being better educated than the masses were prone to organize around secret societies, such as Masonic Orders, Odd Fellows, black Elks, fraternities or sororities and the Masonics to be honored by special services in community churches where they were praised for their achievements before the colonized community. Social events were often presented and the community in general was invited to ogle and pay homage to those who considered themselves the model of society. Black newspapers donated enormous amounts of print to debutante balls and other events that further reenforced the distinction between the intermediary class and the masses of oppressed. The traditional colonized bourgeoisie's efforts to emulate the oppressor's culture often led to imitation of some of the more decadent characteristics of that culture. If their actions are viewed in the context of internal colonization, they are understandable although they may not be understood when they attempt to prove that they are equal to their oppressors in morality and virtue.

The mechanization of the agricultural industry in rural America forced many blacks into the urban centers of this country in the post World War II period. They arrived in urban areas in such large numbers that traditional black institutions that had performed well in the pre-war days were overwhelmed and unprepared to minister to their needs or provide the necessary leadership to modernize those who were basically technological illiterates. Blacks found that many of the benefits of modernization was absorbed by European immigrants, who were unsympathetic and insensitive to the needs of blacks, prior to their arrival on the urban scene. It was clear to the new migrants that adherence to traditional values and the protestant ethic would permanently deny them the fruits of an advanced modern society. From the viewpoint of the black urban masses this was an intolerable situation when their contributions to the nation since its inception was considered.

The new urban blacks were systematically excluded from participation in the fullness of American life by the deliberate tactics of the dominate society. They were discriminated against in employment, trade unions and apprenticeship programs. In the field of education, their schools were inferior and de facto segregated. Adequate housing was non-existent or priced beyond the means of the average Afro-American migrant. They were often treated brutally by the various law enforcement agencies and generally ignored by municipal and federal agencies. The black upper-class tended to remain aloof from these masses who were unskilled and unsophisticated in coping with the dynamics of automation and modernization. In many cases they adopted the attitude of the dominate society and labeled this group of technological misfits as lazy and untrustworthy. It was difficult for those among the black elite group, who had achieved their relatively secure positions in the colonial system through hard work and thrift to identify with this uneducated group who in many instances articulated values that were contrary to their ethical system.

Among the principles of the new urban group espoused was that by virtue of their citizenship, government had a right to ensure equality in all political and economic areas. It was the duty of the society to care for and train the unemployed. It was the duty of government to provide adequate housing and eradicate segregation. It was the duty of government to secure equal educational opportunities and when necessary any additional training that would prepare a citizen for a functional life in America. To the extent that government and the colonized bourgeoisie did not speak to the needs of this urban group, they were derelict and unworthy. Individual initiative was still a major ingredient of this value system, but society's obligations were paramount. If the traditional intermediaries' positions were to continue to be legitimized by the masses, they would have to take a position consistent with the viewpoint of these new migrants.

The position of the masses on inherent rights, the obligations of government and in some instances, the negation of the notions of the protestant ethic was in open conflict with the teachings and principles of the intermediary group and many in government. The masses in frustration took their protest, often violent, into the streets before the watchful eyes of the world through the mass media. Indeed petitions were filed with the United Nations and foreign powers were informed of the plight of the black masses in America. Of the two groups, government and traditional black bourgeoisie, government was the first to recognize the validity of the arguments of the masses. The government did not move with any sense of compassion, but the dynamics of internal colonization dictates that the colonized masses should be complacent or at the very least non-violent. The relationship of the colonizer and the colonized is so close that it is in government's best interest to provide albeit grudgingly, sufficient economic and social mobility to the colonized to ensure the integrity of the system.

The danger to the colonial system was apparent as agitation increased propelling new spokesmen to positions of prominence. There was never any doubt of the government's ability to forcefully suppress internal disorders but there was serious questions as regards their willingness to pay the price of suppression in terms of international prestige, imperialism and white racial privilege. The government's position was further complicated by liberal and radical segments of the dominant community who joined in the protest for better opportunities for oppressed minorities. Many in this group suffered greatly for their advocation of a more egalitarian society. It was clear to the leaders of government that traditional methods of coping with the problems of the minorities would no longer placate the aroused oppressed groups. The trickling down approach through traditional intermediaries was simply dysfunctionaal and could not meet the needs of a majority of the blacks. It was therefore necessary to devise another conduit to funnel the necessities of life to the oppressed.

Time became increasingly important as urban riots wrecked the country from coast to coast. Traditional leaders of upper-class activist organizations, such as the National Association for the Advancement of Colored People and the National Urban League, were unable to contain the black protest. Increasingly, the minorities were expressing their discontent with their legalistic approach to orderly racial improvement. The foundations of the right to govern were being called into question and threatened by this disenchanted group of minorities and liberal-radical whites. It was apparent that any effective acts of government to ameliorate oppression would have to be taken outside of the traditional system, through different intermediaries. To accomplish their objective of restoring some semblance of security, a new elite would be necessary who was sensitive to the viewpoint of the colonized masses and could speak to the needs of both government and the minorities. Of course, these actions on the part of government were resented by traditional organizations who had been active in the field of civil rights for many years as monies were to be channeled around them to others. This necessity brought onto the urban scene a new class of intermediaries who were not bound to traditional concepts and could respond to the imperatives of the new social situation in urban centers.

David Apter describes this new elite who plays a major role in both colonialism and modernization as follows:

"The only other group ... who also were encouraged by the British, were educated and responsible elites. Mostly trained in Britain, or else professional men of one sort or another, they formed a group attempting clearly to play roles assigned in terms of Western education, dress, behavior patterns, values and religion. These were the people whose affiliations were to municipalities, to the detribalized, urbanized, restive and aggressive Westernized society of the Coast."[46]

In Africa, this new elite had strong ties with the traditional elite. Indeed, it was these ties that suggested to the British they would be useful in modernizing traditional societies. With the industrialization of colonial economics and migration of large numbers to urban centers, the colonializing agencies felt traditional leaders were unable to provide the leadership required by a modern situation. Therefore, they looked to this new urban social class for leadership of the masses.

The new urban elite could serve three purposes. Through their ties with the traditional elites, the chiefs and religious leaders could be pacified for their lack of control, because many of them were their sons and relatives. Sec ondly, the new elite class could provide some direction for the masses, who were leaving the tribal preserves and could educate them to the degree required by the colonizers, creating a functional labor force for an industrial economy. Thirdly, through conspicuous consumption, they could provide models for the masses to emulate. This latter function was their principal appeal to their urban constituents. In the process of socializing the masses, they were to instill values and norms consistent with the wishes of the colonializing power. The overall effects of this maneuver would increase the control of Western powers over the colonialized peoples, while giving them a certain amount of power and a part in their own oppression.

An understanding of the nature of this modernizing elite is crucial to an understanding of the colonialization process in Africa and America in the Twentieth Century. This class was a decisive factor in the colonization process and the subsequent fights for liberation. The elite class was elitist, in the sense that they acted in accordance with their definition of class and held certain key positions between colonial powers and the masses. Their educational and cultural ties were with Western Europe. They intermarried or married Europeans and sent their children to European schools. Further, they had the same associational ties with churches and fraternities.

It was only after the masses became restless and aware of the disparity between their economic condition and the ruling classes, that this African bourgeois developed a social consciousness that was to shake the vast European empires. This consciousness led to the formation of mass political parties in nearly all African countries. These parties led by professional groups agitated until freedom was achieve and they have played a valuable role in the Africanization of the former colonies.

In America, the colonializing power has followed nearly the same model of action. When agitation for civil rights increased to embarrassing proportions in the 1960's, the federal and some state governments moved to establish a new modernizing elite to oversee the problems and concerns of the colonized poor, especially black Americans. This was done through the establishment of a War on Poverty Program and other urban projects, that was to administer to all of the needs of the blacks in the fields of medical care, manpower training, housing and other economic, legal and social needs.

The War on Poverty Program was so large that a new urban elite or group was necessary to administer it. This elite was formed by raising the economic and social levels of a few blacks to dominance over others. This elite was developed in many ways distinct and divorced from the traditional black elite who had for many years fought to achieve the aspirations of a colonized people. This new elite did not have the traditional institutional basis of authority normally respected in the black community, that is, it did not have the black church, educational institutions or traditional civil rights organizations as a basis of legitimacy. Their legitimacy and authority were derived directly from the colonializing power as a means of placating and neutralizing the disruptive behavior of the alienated.

The new elites are often technocrats who are seemingly faceless in the black community. They are skilled in community organization, manpower development, public health, urbal relations, public administration, housing and other fields of specialization that are useful in urban development. They are bureaucrats who are capable of manipulating bureaucricies for the benefit of their constituencies. They balance and allocate the resources of government to meet the needs of the oppressed community. In an industrial society, the task of training and assisting those who have difficulty in the internal modernization of the colonized is largely their responsibility.[47]

Establishment of the new elite of the past decade served the colonizers well. It accomplished at least three things. Firstly, it delayed or stopped the violent revolts that were occurring in the streets. Secondly, it soothed the conscience of the dominating population to the extent civil rights agitation is no longer considered a valid exercise of the colonized people. Thirdly, it divided the leadership of the poor blacks in America, making them more manageable and less a threat to the ruling power.

What followed was predictable. Today, as in the last days of colonialism in Africa, we find blacks in confrontation with other blacks, Chicanos in confrontation with Chicanos, blacks in confrontation with Chicanos, and poor whites accusing blacks and Chicanos of footdragging, laziness and immorality. The effect of this has been to remove the focus of attention to the colonized people themselves.

Dr. Andrew F. Brimmer, in the New York Times, spoke to the seriousness of the division that is artificially being created among the black people in the United States:

"A leading Negro economist predicted here today that it would be 'quite some time' before there would be any improvement in the employment situation for black Americans."

"Dr. Andrew F. Brimmer, the lone black member of the board of governors of the Federal Reserve System, said the picture was not so bleak that many blacks had 'given up' and no longer even bothered to enter the labor force."

"Dr. Brimmer ... said that while the 'vast proportion of black people still do not have marketable skills,' others were doing 'reasonably well.'"

"This is why I am afraid of a schism among blacks developing," he declared. "If you go through and look at what has been happening in some professional categories and so on, a handful of black people have moved ahead."[48]

Dr. Brimmer's fears, in my opinion, are justified. The colonizers continue to hold the real power and allocates only as much to the new elite as is necessary to accomplish the purposes previously mentioned. Apparently, there was no genuine concern on the part of the colonizers to raise the standards of living for all poor people or to provide maximum civil liberties to all of the citizens. We have witnessed the exercise of this power through the removal of members of this new elite, whose legitimacy is based on the authority of the ruling powers, when their actions are contradictory to the expectations of the colonializers. Further, we have noticed the cleavage which is quite analogous to the African situation, between this elite and the traditional black American elite.

Information Relative to the Current State of Internal Modernization

The colonialized, black man's progress toward modernization has not proceeded without many difficulties created by institutionalized racism. His just and moral fight for equality has taken place on legislative, judicial and executive battle-grounds on this system. As of this date, there is no national commitment to bring him into the mainstream of American society by eliminating poverty and offering all citizens an equal opportunity to participate in the promise of this nation.

The urbanization process, a part of the modernization process, has brought additional social problems that impede the progress of blacks. Blacks are usually forced by their economic situation to live in a substandard environment with little possibility of acquiring the skills necessary to compete in American society. In spite of the progress reported by Franklin and others, we are still faced with the following environmental problems in large urban centers across the nation.

This is a brief description of an urban ghetto in 1971:

"The community itself, Lawndale, is very much like any other black section of a major American city. About 180,000 people crowd into its 12 square miles. Whether it is called a ghetto or a community, the visible symbols remain the same: the sense of Elizabethan vitality and forment painfully contrasting with the physical reality of spiritually dead loafers in colorful habits decorating the fronts of bars and stores and barbershops; children darting in and out of these shops or playing in gutters; mother hauling plastic sacks of clothes to and from laundromats, young women looking vacantly nowhere. The radio music which keeps it all alive blares into the street, sometimes overpowered by bullvoiced disc jockeys hawking care and clothes and color television. Older women look down on the street, watching the children and just watching; a repossession notice, from downtown floats along the pavement on the wind. The stylized movements of eyes and fingers and feet; the screaming colors; the pictures and posters of this year's politicians sloppily posted over those from last year; the bourbon billboards, the uncleared lots and falling houses bearing graffiti of resident groups - Vice Lords, Conservative Vice Lords, Disciples, Black Panthers. The storefront churches; the other houses struggling to survive; the sense of having seen it all or of having read about it all someplace before."[49]

The inner-city ghettos exist as part of the urban environment and are surrounded by affluent white residential and financial districts. These conditions exist in areas where the ghetto residents can easily compare their deprived conditions to that of the wealthy. It is in these districts that the black urban elite exercise their control and attempt to bring about modernization. This situation points to the schism among blacks spoken of by Brimmer. Clearly, a small number of people from the ghetto have risen above this class and moved on to the white suburbs that ring Chicago and other major cities. The lack of national commitment to eliminate all poverty has left the citizens of these ghettos to fend for themselves with little in the way of operational tools that would enable them to find a niche in the ongoing process of modernization.

The social environment described above has led to the advocation of radical changes within our society that are clearly divisive. For instance, a prominent black jurist, Judge William T. Hustie, relates that an alarming number of Negroes "accept and encourage racial separation as a desirable and potentially rewarding way of American life." He said that "the separatist attitude had been created in part by a system that locked millions of poor blacks into overcrowded center city slums."[50]

A prerequisite for changing the foregoing situation and stimulating internal modernization is an intellectual and political elite dedicated to the articulation and implementation of policies that transform the traditional society. Since this elite, given internal colonialism, is necessarily small we find the effects of modernization contradictory. It is both integrative, and in the case of traditional societies disintegrative. The process is so dynamic that often values are formed well after behavior has been established. Indeed, seldom do two elements of society adapt themselves at the same rate causing disorders, violence or peculiar forms of adaptive behavior unacceptable either to traditional forces or new modernizing leaders.[51]

In order to bring about this change in leadership, a change in institutions is necessary. In the context of black America, E. Franklin Frazier has indicated this internal modernization process was disruptive and was primarily responsible for the large migration of rural blacks to urban centers in the North and South. This migration created a rupture between individuals and their traditional institutions, such as the family and church. Frazier found that the black church, in the urban environment, for many years served as an integrative factor in the lives of the new urbanites. It gave them cohesion and identity.[52]

These institutional changes proceed unevenly. Smelser says:

"A modernizing country, then displays a multiplicity of institutional changes; and no matter how carefully social change is planned some institutional changes will always lead the way, and others will always lag behind. Thus a developing nation, if it could be depicted graphically, would resemble a large, awkward animal lumbering forward by moving each of its parts, sometimes in partial coordination and sometimes in opposition to one another."[53]

It is germane to this discussion to indicate what progress, if any, has been made in the black Americans' quest for modernization. In this case I am speaking of progress for the total colonialized black community, rather than the exceptional progress made by a few as previously related.

In politics in 1940, "politically, the Negro was totally powerless in the South before the war--he was barred by the white primary rule of the democratic parties. Fewer than 100,000 Negroes in the South are estimated to have voted in the general elections of 1940."[54] A 1944 Supreme Court decision struck down the white primary. However, in 1971, Clarence Mitchell, Chief lobbiest on Capitol Hill reported--"In the past, we never had this problem under Republicans or Democrats--getting governmental backing on the right to vote. But even this year we are still on the battlefield trying to make sure the law is enforced."[55] The unequal enforcement of laws and failure to guarantee civil rights in relation to the colonized are tools of the colonizer. These tools are used to keep minority groups in an inferior position both politically and economically.

In the area of employment, in 1940, twenty-six unions in the American Federation of Labor had clauses in their constitutions explicitly barring Negro members. Even in the federal government, with few exceptions, only menial work was open to Negroes. In 1960 it was reported that blacks continued to face severe union discrimination in such large areas of the economy as the building trades and railroads. White collar and managerial jobs remained closed to blacks in the South and to some extent elsewhere; only 12 percent of Black men in the country had such positions, against 40 percent for white workers. In the recession of 1957-1958, 19.8 percent of the blacks in the labor force were unemployed. There has been some progress made in certain areas as indicated in Chapter 1, but the overall picture is not very good.[56]

Herbert Hills, a member of the National Association for the Advancement of Colored People's National Labor Division and his remarks on the problem of employment of black people in 1971 are informative. They indicate that the colonized people have made little progress in this area in the past decade. He asserts,

"... the government through failure to enforce compliance with laws that
prohibit discrimination in employment, was directly subsidizing racial
discrimination in employment to the extent of billions of dollars of
public funds every year ... The rate of unemployment for black workers
in 25 major centers of urban non-white population was not less than 25
to 40 percent and that the unemployment rate for black ghetto youth would
be in excess of 50 percent by mid-summer. This development is the single
most volatile factor in causing urban unrest and holds explosive implications for the future stability of American society."[57]

The United States Census Bureau verified the statement of Hill. It reports that
one-third of the nation's twenty-three million blacks or seven and one half million
live on incomes below the national poverty level in 1971. This figure is higher than
the 7.2 million that was below this level in 1969.[58]

The foregoing political and economic situations are compounded by a lack of
commitment, on the part of the federal government, to quality education for the
colonized minorities. Mrs. June Shsgaloff Alexander, director of Education for
the National Association for the Advancement of Colored People says, "previously
this administration consistently failed to provide leadership for the country in
ending segregated schools."[59]

In Gary T. Marx's cross sectional study on the climate of opinions on civil
rights in 1964, he found in response to the question "Do you think that in general
things are getting better or getting worse for Negroes in this country?" that most
blacks considered the position of Negroes in the society was improving.[60] The
elites in this sample responded to a similar question as follows:

Table 12

POSITION OF BLACKS

Reply to: "In your opinion, has the position of blacks in America been rapidly improving, mildly improving, worse or essentially the same as it was during World War
II?"

	Traditional Elites (percent)	New Urban Elites (percent)
Rapidly improving	23	14
Mildly improving	60	60
Worse	3	5
Same	9	9
No response	5	12
Total	100	100

The difference in perceptions on improvement of blacks (the traditional elites
83% improving and the new urban elites 74% improving) are pronounced. Although both

groups overwhelmingly indicate the conditions of blacks are improving political leaders can take little satisfaction in this fact when action is considered in race relations. After the study by Marx in 1964 which clearly indicated the same trend some of the greatest racial conflicts in the history of this country occurred. It seems to be the case that the rate of change is a causative variable in social disorders rather than an indicator of concrete change although they are somewhat interrelated. For instance, only twenty-three percent (23%) of the traditional elites and fourteen percent (14% of the new urban elites felt that conditions for blacks in America were rapidly improving. It is with the large number of blacks who perceive their situation as mildly improving that there is likely to be agitation for an increase in the rate of progress and discontent with the prevailing political, social and economic order. The greater the perception of improvement the more rapidly change and equality will be demanded.

Racism and the Internal Modernization Process

Any discussion of the racial situation in America that does not include some aspects of white racism would be incomplete. There is no other element as tenacious or pervasive in American interrelationships as racism. Joel Kovel has indicated that in America, white racism is no aberration. It is an ingredient of our culture.[61] White racism is the cement that binds together the colonial system and white privilege. It is irrational, dehumanizing and oppressive. When racism is utilized to systematically dominate minorities through institutions and government, it has an appearance of rationality and is perceived as such from time to time. However, when it is analyzed closely it is apparent that it is based upon opportunism and white privilege.

Racism is an ingredient of the colonial culture but it is also true that the human organism can act out against cultural variables. Racism is a deliberate variable in human behavior and is used to achieve predetermined objectives, both psychological and material. Blauner points out that the colonial system in America buttressed by white racism, permits white Americans to enjoy special privileges in all areas of existence where racial minorities are systematically excluded or disadvantaged. These areas include housing and neighborhoods, education, income and life style. It can be demonstrated that there are those in the dominant race who would surrender their positions of privilege but the internal modernization of blacks is deliberately controlled by the colonizers among them to enhance this system of privilege that the dominant race enjoys, and it pervades all of their institutions.[62]

Albert Memmi points out that as regards colonial groupings, all efforts of the colonialist are directed toward maintaining social immobility, and racism is the surest weapon for this aim. In effect, change becomes impossible, and any revolt would be absurd.[63] He further indicates that,

> "Racism appears then, not as an incidental detail, but as a cosubstantial part of colonialism. It is the highest expression of the colonial system and one of the most significant features of the colonialist. Not only does it establish a fundamental discrimination between colonizer and colonized, a sine qua non of colonial life, but it also lays the foundation for the immutability of this life.[64]

While racism in its psychological and institutional dimension is resistant to change, the goal it serves is white privilege and gives the colonized a viable instrument to relatively improve their standards of existence in the oppressive system with a limited degree of internal modernization. A functional, complacent colonized group is essential to white racial privilege. This colonized group must be brought into the modernization process to a limited degree to ensure the position of white privilege. If a colonized group is totally dysfunctional to the colonizer then the colonizer either liquidates this group or withdraws from the relationship. However, the psychological benefits of racism mitigates against a complete destruction of the colonial relationship.

The colonizer is skillful in the manipulation of a system of rewards, punishments and limited mobility. Through this system he is able to control the colonized with a limited expenditure of resources. Although the colonized have very little positive power, they do have a certain degree of negative power in the sense that upon a given occasion they can deny the colonizer his position of privilege. A decision of this kind is usually executed at a great deal of suffering and denial on the part of the colonized, but it seems to be the only effective way of achieving a limited amount of control within the framework of internal colonialism.

Essentially, the colonized must raise the level of tension surrounding the cleavage between the colonizer and the colonized to the point where the colonizer considers it is in his best interest (i.e., the maintenance of racial privilege) to ameliorate the differences between the two groups. The urban rebellions of the last decade are indicative of this tactic. The colonizer, prior to the rebellions, refused to admit that many of the problems articulated by the leaders of these urban uprisings existed. The colonizer's response to this action on the part of the colonized was a War on Poverty program administered through a new group of intermediaries, that proved to be totally inadequate to solve the consequences of racism, but adequate enough to temporarily arrest the immediate threat against the colonial system of white privileges.

The nature of racism in a colonial situation is such that it is impossible for the colonizer to impute to the colonized masses the ability to determine that rather than live in rat infested tenements they would prefer to burn them down. The colonizer could not accept that perhaps the destruction of the enterprises that exploited blacks in their neighborhoods could be a deliberate act on the part of the colonized and a method of heightening tensions to a degree that would benefit the colonized. The colonizer found it difficult to admit that many of the participants in these rebellions were basically hard working and fairly secure, by colonial standards, subjects of the system. The colonizer preferred to categorize these rebels as the lawless element of the subordinate group. They were to be considered the irresponsible elements of the black community whose sole motives were looting and self gain.

The colonizers actions and the seemingly coordinated nature of the eruptions, clearly indicates that although he created a false image of the character of the rebellious participants, the colonizer was under no illusions as to the true nature of the actions of the oppressed. There was a degree of sophistication in these rebellions that pointed to the modernization of elements within the colonized community, particularly in the areas of community organization and political action. While condemning the rebels as lawless and without any substantial voice in the black community, the colonizer moved to meet some of the needs of this group by the establishment of programs especially for the benefit of the rebels.

The colonizer has been able to reverse many of the emergency actions taken during this tempestuous period largely because the majority of white Americans seemingly are willing to accept his notion that blacks are irresponsible, unworthy and not imbued with the same human characteristics imputed to members of the dominate race. Since the riots were carried out by a lawless element of the black community, there should be more stringent and punitive laws to control those who are lazy, shiftless, dishonest and seeking only handouts. To impute to the colonized the noble notions of preferring death to subjugation or physical discomfort to racial humiliation and denial of manhood would give the colonized a dignity that equals or surpasses his own. The colonized woujd no longer be a thing to be manipulated strictly in terms of racial privilege but rather a human being with certain inalienable human rights. One of the more important aspects of human rights is the right to be free and to exercise all of the perogatives of a free person.

To substantiate his argument that the rebellions were carried out by a lawless element of the colonized community, the colonizer was able to point to a significant degree of progress achieved by blacks since World War II. For instance, in the field of housing it could be pointed out that home ownership in the black community had increased three percent between 1950 and 1960. The colonizer does not point out that home ownership for whites during the same period had increased seven percent. Further, the coloni-er failed to draw attention to the fact that between 1960 and 1966, 2.4 million blacks moved into the already crowded and deteriorating urban ghetto after being forced out of their rural environment by automation.[65]

The colonizer could draw attention to the fact that in 1960 almost all black children 7 to 13 years old were enrolled in the nation's school system, whereas twenty years ago, one in five were not. Yet the colonizer will fail to point out that the modest progress that took place in the 1950's reached a virtual standstill and actual reversals in educational opportunities for blacks began at the close of the 1960's. Desegregation of public schools in the South almost ceased; between 1954 and 1957, 7.1 school districts desegregated; in 1958 the number dropped to 13; to 19 in 1959 and 17 in 1960.[66]

In terms of income it could be pointed out that between 1949 and 1964 the median annual income for non-white families went from $1,650 to $3,800. However, the colonizer could be relied upon not to point out that these gains compared with an increase in white income from $3,200 to $6,800 during the same period.[67] For aggregate income in 1948: white income was $146.2 billion, non-white income $7.9 billion, a difference of $1,38.3 billion; by 1963 white income was $347.5 billion while black income was $23.6 billion, a difference that expanded to $232.0 billion.[68]

The colonizers have been able to convince themselves that attempts to remedy the inequities between races in terms of financial support for agencies such as the Office of Economic Opportunity is a wasteful expenditure of their resources. In spite of the many successes of these agencies in the fields of job training, education, housing redevelopment and others the colonizers have elected to reverse the moderate interest previously exhibited in bettering the conditions of the poor. The results of these cutbacks in services to the poor will be to force the new urban elites out of their leadership position and a return to dealing with the minorities through traditional elites whom they trust.

The colonizers, through the Office of Economic Opportunity for a period of several years gave a push to the internal modernization process. They indicated an awareness that the urban centers were no longer a place of opportunity where all could come and provided they had initiative, the migrants could achieve. It recognized the agreements of the new elite and black masses that government has a paramount obligation to provide for its citizens a minimum standard of training, employment, housing and medical care to enable them to become functional in an industrial nation. However, when the operation of these agencies are viewed from the perspective of the average colonizer as a useless expenditure of money for an undeserving group of people who are poor because of their own actions, the minorities are forced into the vicious cycle of poverty and colonialism that denies them opportunities for training and education; deny them jobs because they lack training and education; stigmatize them as inferior and lazy because they cannot secure jobs because they lack training and education and are forced to live on the doles the majority community chooses to dispense. Their actions based upon race reinforces their position of privilege and superiority and justifies their domination through the internal colonial process.

An example of the magnitude of this reversal in policy can be observed in Oakland, California where 1.8 million dollars are expected to be cut from funds for schools in areas such as special education and extra funds to educate children from military reservations. An additional 2.1 million dollars is to be cut from programs administered by the school system.[69]

It is expected that 1.8 million dollars will be cut from the Neighborhood Development program that provides urban renewal in North and East Oakland. 1.2 to 2.2 million dollars are to be cut from the West Oakland Model Cities program where 45 percent of the residents have incomes below the poverty level. The Emergency Employment Act is not expected to be funded. It had a 3.4 million dollar program. 1.5 million dollars for federally assisted code enforcement which provide money for people to fix up old homes to meet the city's safety and health codes will not be funded.[70]

In the areas of employment and job training $778,608 was expected to be cut from the summer job program in 1973 cutting the number of available jobs from 3,400 to 2,000. All funding for Public Service Careers, a $214,250 program is to be eliminated. The $143,500 year-round Neighborhood Youth Corps will no longer be funded. A $11,000, cut from the 1.8 million dollar annual budget of the Concentrated Employment Program which among other things provides finances for job training was expected in 1973.[71]

The racist connotations to this reversal in policy are emphasized by the fact that the minority population, mostly black, is forty-one percent of the city's population officially, although there are estimates that place the minority population as high as fifty-five percent. Seventy-nine percent of the school population consists of minorities and cuts in education and training funds affect them directly. Redevelopment and Code Enforcement funding were used in the flatland area where most of the minorities reside.

Racism in the framework of internal modernization impedes the industrialization of the masses. However, due to the close demographic proximity of the colonizer and the colonized, a moderate degree of internal modernization is in the best interest of the colonizer. The oppression suffered by minority groups leads to the constant changing of institutions in the colonized community to offset the effects of the actions of the colonizer. This is especially true in the field of politics where in recent years black caucuses have been formed for concerted action and a national political party is beginning to articulate the objectives and needs of the oppressed. The internal modernization of the colonized community will be tolerated when it can be controlled and serves to reinforce the position of privilege enjoyed by the dominant community.

Conclusion

In this section internal modernization was discussed as a process that evolves when traditional institutions and values of a people are destroyed by the revolutionary nature of internal colonization. It develops partly through the desires of the colonized to master the technology of the colonizing power to avoid the degradation of colonization and partly because traditional institutions were incapable of competing with advance technology.

The socio-psychological impact of colonization and African residuals were reviewed in terms of their roles in the internal modernization of blacks. It has been indicated that in internal colonization the oppressed often take on many of the characteristics of the oppressor. This imitation of the colonizer leads to a modification of behavior and value systems that stimulate racial advancement in terms of achievement in the new industrial environment. This has been a continuous process from the earliest days of the black man's existence on this continent. This limitation has not been limited to technology but has extended to other areas. Many of the colonized accepted the colonizer's premise on the lightness of skin. In the colonized community skin color at one time was as important as in the dominant community with the result that darker skin blacks were discriminated against in both the great community and his own colonized community. The result of this phenomenon was that in terms of internal modernization the darker skinned blacks were the last to enter the process.

When rural black populations migrated to the urban centers they found that political and economic mobility were to be denied to them. The ideas and institutions that served the European immigrant so well in integrating into American society were guarded jealously by this group. Not the least among these political resources that were available to many Northern European ethnics was the unreformed municipal governments which permitted ethnic groups to receive patronage and give them an input into the political process. Although some European ethnics were able to utilize this system for political, economic and social advancement, blacks were the last major ethnic group to migrate to the urban centers to be confronted with their alleged ineffectiveness and corruption. Instead of being able to avail themselves of this instrument of political participation, blacks were forced to live under the reformed type of municipal administration that catered to the needs of the wealthy and powerful at the expense of the poor who had no voice in shaping their destinies. As blacks begin to gain some control of local politics through increases in urban population, their political power is to be further nullified by the regional reorganization of municipal governments.

The internal modernization of the black minority was led by an activist elite that served as intermediaries between the colonizer and the colonized. There is a traditional elite that largely adheres to the principles of the protestant ethnic and capitalism. It emphasizes hard work, thrift and gradualism in the solution of racial problems. It is led by conservative organizations such as the National Association for the Advancement of Colored Peoples and the National Urban League whose membership has a middle-class base as indicated in Chapter 1 and tends to interact with fraternities, sororities, masonics and other organizations that may have a vested interest in the framework of internal colonization because the model legitimizes their roles as elites in the colonized communities. This elite of upper-classes has served the masses well in the past because it was largely through their efforts that whatever progress the colonized achieved prior to the mid-twentieth century was through their efforts and leadership. Their influence based on past performance is a significant factor in the black community.

The migration of large numbers of blacks to the urban centers overwhelmed the institutions and indigenous leadership who had little experience in coping with the problems posed by this migration. This led to social disruption and a new group of technocrats and bureaucrats evolved to stabilize the situation and bring about social order. This group is defined as experts in community organizing, housing, education, health and other fields that performed a direct service to the oppressed. Usually they did not have the same associational ties of the traditionals and were more attuned to the urban needs of the black masses. Since they were legitimized by the dominate community rather than the colonized after their objectives were achieved.

Both psychological and institutional racism plays an important part in the process of internal modernization. Both business and labor have exploited the minority races. The government of the colonizer has used racist methods through their institutions and the media to demean the efforts of the colonized masses to achieve relative parity. All of the major institutions of the colonizer's community were mobilized to stigmatize the minorities, in an attempt to prove them unworthy and undeserving. This was done in a large measure to enhance white privilege and the average colonial quickly accepted this method of protecting their positions. The psychological myth that imputes inhumane characteristics to people of color is the basis of institutional racism that con-rols the progress of minorities as they attempt to enter the mainstream of industrialization.

In the following chapter the attitudes of the colonized elite, both traditional and the new elites will be explored to determine their perceptions of their society. Contrary to the rhetoric of some of the radicals, black and white, there is evidence that indicates in the realm of interaction between the races a large number of the colonized minorities look to this group for leadership. To the extent that they are perceived as leaders by the masses, their actions have a direct bearing on the responses of the colonized to their situation and is therefore sociologically relevant.

REFERENCES TO CHAPTER 3

1. The Oakland Sunshine, December 27, 1913, p. 1.

2. Gino Germani, Secularization, Modernization and Economic Development in the Protestant Ethnic and Modernization, ed. Eisenstady, S. N. (New York: Basic Books, Inc., Publishers) 1968, pp. 279-281.

3. Martin Kilson, Political Change in a West African State (Cambridge: Harvard University Press, 1966), pp. 7-8.

4. Ibid., p. 37.

5. Karl Deutsen, Social Mobilization and Political Development, Wilbert E. Moore and Neil J. Smelser, eds., "Modernization of Traditional Societies (Englewood Cliffs, Prentice Hall, Inc., 1966) p. 2.

6. Ibid.

7. William H. Friedland, A Sociological Approach to Modernization (Ithaca: Cornell University Press, 1969) pp. 35-37.

8. Genovese, Eugene D., An Encounter on the Origins of Black Nationalism, in Black Liberation Politics, ed., Edward Greer (Boston: Allyn and Bacon, Inc., 1971) p. 44.

9. Elkins, Stanley M., Slavery (Chicago: University of Chicago Press, 1959) p. 115.

10. Ibid., pp. 90-91.

11. Ibid., p. 96.

12. Ibid., pp. 97-98.

13. John Hope Franklin, From Slavery to Freedom (New York: Alfred A. Knopf, 1967) p. 119.

14. Elkins, op. cit., p. 81.

15. Ibid., pp. 101-103.

16. C. E. Black, The Dynamics of Modernization (New York: Harper and Row, Publishers, 1967) p. 9.

17. Franklin, op. cit., pp. 232-233.

18. Ibid.

19. Ibid., p. 272.

20. Ibid., p. 389.

21. Ibid., p. 391.

22. Ibid., p. 393.

23. William Loren Katz, Eyewitness: The Negro in American History (New York: Pitman Publishing Corp., 1968) pp. 295-305.

24. Ibid.

25. Franklin, op. cit., pp. 578-579.

26. Ibid.

27. Alfred H. Kelly and Winifred A. Harbison, The American Constitution, Its Origin and Development (New York: W. W. Norton & Company, 1963) pp. 407-452.

28. Ibid., p. 457.

29. Ibid., p. 461.

30. Ibid., p. 1014.

31. Franklin, op. cit., p. 306.

32. Ibid.

33. Ibid.

34. Ibid., p. 309.

35. Ibid., p. 310.

36. Ibid., pp. 312-313.

37. St. Clair Drake and Horace R. Cayton, Black Metropolis (New York: Harcourt, Brace and World, Inc., 1962) pp. 661-662.

38. Ibid., p. 527.

39. Ibid.

40. Ibid., p. 525.

41. Winthrop Jordan, White Over Black (Baltimore: Penguin Books, Inc., 1969) pp. 139-141.

42. Frazier, op. cit., p. 27.

43. Drake and Clayton, op. cit., p. 531.

44. St. Clair Drake and Horace R. Cayton, op. cit., p. 212.

45. Ibid., p. 539.

46. David E. Apter, Ghana in Transition (New York: Atheneum Press, 1958) p. 148.

47. Joel Kovel, White Racism (New York: Vintage Books, 1970) p. 3.

48. The New York Times, Vol. CXX, July 8, 1971, p. 10.

49. James Alan McPhersen, The Story of the Contract Ruyers League, the Atlantic, April, 1972, Vol. 229, No. 4, p. 52.

50. The New York Times, Vol. CXX, July 8, 1971, p. 1.

51. Black, op. cit., p. 9.

52. E. Franklin Frazier, The Negro Church (New York: Antheneum Press, 1948) p. 81.

53. Neil J. Smelser, The Modernization of Social Relations in Modernization, ed. Myron Weiner (New York Basic Books, 1966) pp. 111-112.

54. The New York Times, Section IV, dated March 10, 1960, p. 10.

55. The New York Times, CXX, dated July 9, 1972, p. 8.

56. Ibid.

57. The New York Times, F 14, VI, May 10, 1960, p. 10.

58. The San Francisco Chronicle, July 13, 1972, p. 10.

59. The New York Times, CXX, July 9, 1971.

60. Gary T. Marx, Protest and Prejudice (New York: Harper and Row Publishers, 1967) pp. 106-125.

61. Blauner, Racial Oppression in America, op. cit., p. 2.

62. Ibid.

63. Memmi, op. cit., p. 74.

64. Ibid.

65. Willhelm, op. cit., pp. 109-113.

66. Ibid., p. 115.

67. U.S. News and World Report, War on Poverty, Vol. LXXV, No. 21, May 21, 1973, pp. 68-69.

68. Ibid.

69. Ibid.

70. Ibid.

71. Ibid.

Chapter 4

ATTITUDES OF THE OAKLAND BLACK BOURGEOISIE

The preceding chapters were primarily addressed to an analysis of the Oakland black bourgeoisie within the framework of internal colonization and modernization. One of the questions with which this study began concerns the more general attitudes of the elite toward problems confronting the black community. What are the problems of pressing importance to the community as seen from the middle-class perspective?

General Impressions Regarding Problems in the Community

On many occasions the dominant community has been accused of failure in understanding the needs of the black community, i.e, they are not aware of the communities perceptions of their needs before acting in a given situation. One of the responses to this criticism has been that the black community is too disorganized and there is no general consensus among blacks as to their needs. The data clearly indicates the invalidity of this response although there are differences in defining their needs between traditional elites and new urban elites and it is only a question of degree.

Recent reports indicate there has been a significant increase in the use of illegal drugs or narcotics in the black community. Indeed, some black militants consider this increase in illegal drug activity as a deliberate mechanism on the part of the dominant power structure to make Afro-Americans a docile, pliable and non-agitating element of the society. Table 2 indicates the response of the middle-class as to the effectiveness of law enforcement agencies in the suppression of this illegal traffic ...

Table 13

ILLEGAL DRUGS

Reply to: "Do you think the narcotic problem is handled well by the police?"

	Traditional Elites (percent)	New Urban Elites (percent)
Handled well by the police	26	17
Not handled well by police	66	77
No response	8	6
Total	100	100

It is apparent that the overwhelming majority of the black middle class feel that the problem of illegal drugs in the black community is not handled well by the local law enforcement personnel. Further, many clearly indicate that they feel there is collusion between these officials and those who profit from this traffic.

Table 14

PROBLEMS IN COMMUNITY

Reply to: "What are the most pressing problems in the black community? Indicate three of those problems."

	Traditional Elites (percent)	New Urban Elites (percent)
Employment and economic factors	57	68
Housing	29	46
Education	20	34
Political awareness	17	26
Lack of black unity	5	14
Drugs or narcotics	5	9
Black community's lack of faith in America	0	5
Others (i.e., religion, prostitution, etc.)	26	8
	(35)	(35)

Most of those who indicated economic factors, employment and poverty were the most pressing problems in the black community felt there was a lack of commitment on the part of the local and Federal governments to eliminate under-employment and unemployment. Recent trends in decreased support for Manpower Training Programs, education, anti-poverty programs and lack of enforcement of anti-bias rules in labor unions were the basis for their conclusions. The purpose is to keep blacks docile and imputes an economic motive to the collusion of police officials and drug operators.

Sample comments:

"Addicts are not identified until they are caught doing wrong."
                                        -Record Shop owner

"Supply dealers pay-off."
                                        -Barbershop owner

"Police use this traffic for their own personal capital gains."
                                        -Teacher

"Yes they cannot really find all of them."
                                        -Liquor Store owner

"Yes: The police are doing their job by following the law. The law needs to be more stringent against narcotics."
                                        -Beauty Shop owner

"Police benefit from this traffic."
                                        -Service Station owner

"Needs black officers to properly handle."
                                        -Security Agency owner

"Drugs are a real problem in any impoverished community. Present police only complicate matters."
-Professor

Since the 1954 United States Supreme Court ruling in Brown vs. Board of Education there have been efforts by some communities to integrate the public school systems. One of the methods that has caused a great deal of controversy is that of busing children to schools that are some distance from their homes. Most of the complaints to this method have been voiced by the white community, however, occasionally blacks and other minority groups, notably the Chinese in San Francisco have resisted efforts to bus their children out of their neighborhoods. Table 3 pertains to this issue.

Table 15

SCHOOL BUSING

Reply to: "There has been a great deal of controversy over busing children to schools. Do you support school busing?"

	Traditional Elites (percent)	New Urban Elites (percent)
Support busing	69	66
Do not support busing	26	23
No response	5	11
Total	100	100

Although there is a majority of middle-class blacks in favor of busing, there appears to be a substantial minority among this group who are opposed to the idea of busing children to school for any reason. Some of the respondents felt that busing children outside of the area of the home removed them further from parents control. Some of the comments that accompanied the responses to this question are:

"The only way schools are going to be integrated."
-Minister

"The problem of education cannot be solved by busing the children from one area to another. The schools' problems are an economic problem and must be improved in home to achieve its goals."
-Personnel Director

"Black community schcols do not meet the needs of the community."
-Minister

"Supports busing - to integrate schools. Residential patterns prevent integration in any other way."
-Dentist

"Supports busing - To keep my children in school, away from some people."
-Plater

"Quality education is what is desired. As long as kids are in separate schools they can be treated differently. When a school gets all black,

certain things happen. I would rather see a racially balanced school.
This issue is clouded. The worst case of busing I have seen is in
Alaska."

-Attorney

Community control of certain functions in the black community has been the focus
of many who feel that the minorities should have more control over agencies that have
a direct effect on their lives. The Black Panther Party and others have felt that
this type control would restore dignity to the ghetto blacks and decrease abuses by
those who enter the community to administer to the oppressed with little knowledge
and sympathy for the different cultural characteristics of the minority communities.

Certainly, few will deny the flagrant abuses of privilege by members of the
police department who often move into minority communities in very much the manner
of an occupying Army. In addition indignities heaped upon those who must receive
public assistance are numerous and these programs are often administered by people
who have a very limited understanding of the nature of a poverty community. Some
blacks have felt that the schools are not fulfilling the needs of their children.
There are high drop-out rates and often those who finish high school are unable to
compete successfully with others who do not attend school in the minority communities. These situations have periodically brought about action on the part of minority
groups for control at the community level.

Table 16

COMMUNITY CONTROL

Reply to: "What is your position on community control of the following functions in
the black community?"

	Traditional Elites (percent)		No Response (percent)	New Urban Elites (percent)		No Response (percent)
	Yes	No		Yes	No	
Police	29	46	25	34	43	23
Welfare	46	26	28	43	40	17
Educational institutions	51	26	23	46	37	17

It is apparent the respondents do not see community control of the police as a
viable means of accomplishing community goals. However, the respondents obviously
believe that community control of welfare and educational institutions would be beneficial and feasible. Some of the responses to this question regarding community
control's positive aspects are as follows:

"Police would be more understanding of the nature of the crime in the
ghetto and try to eliminate it."

-Attorney

"Educational control aid in developing minds of children."

-Teacher

"Help keep people really under control and out of prison."
                              -Plater

"Better relationships as far as police is concerned. Better and more control of the distribution of Welfare funds."
                              -Teacher

"A better understanding and response to the needs of the community."
                              -Nurse

"Nothing - if the tax (dollar) base is weakened. To control a hollow institution is like no control at all."
                              -Educational Administrator

"More sensitivity to the needs of the black populace."
                              -Professor

The Fight for Civil Rights

In the 1970's there has been a noticeable decline in mass confrontation in tactics to gain civil rights for minorities of color. The Federal Administration has
indicated specific actions in this area have been reduced in national priority and
it has been stated that the government should treat these problems with benign neglect. Many of the black middle-class achieved their present positions during the
period of 1963 to 1970, a period of high racial tensions in America, that focused
the attention of the world on the problems resulting from unequal opportunity and
the differences between the values and norms of American society and the actual practices of the dominant race.

This period of turmoil, although agonizing for the entire population, effected
the middle-class or intermediary group of blacks perhaps more than any other group.
This class was called upon to respond to the greater society's demand for control
and the black's demands for leadership simultaneously in an emotionally charged and
violent situation. The traditional elites did not meet the needs satisfactorily of
either group. The power structure in many instances by-passed this group to deal
with new intermediaries that they chose and the black masses put forward. The black
middle-class was in a position of extreme stress.

To some of the participants in the civil rights struggle of all races the achievement of legal or statutory rights and the integration of public accommodations were
the key issues. Others say equality and total integration into the American society
as the key issues of the conflict. The middle class in this study was questioned in
regards to their participation-activism and their perceptions on the achievement of
the goals of the Civil Rights Movement.

Table 17

CIVIL RIGHTS DEMONSTRATIONS

Reply to: "Did you at any time since World War II participate in any marches or demonstrations to secure civil rights for minorities?"

	Traditional Elites (percent)	New Urban Elites (percent)
Participated in demonstrations	63	48
Did not participate in demonstrations	31	48
No response	6	4
Total	100	100

The differences between the two elite groups on this question seems to be related to the differences in their economic base. In some cases the new urban elites indicated to the researcher that employment by the government or other public sector employment moderated and inhibited their actions in terms of overt militant acts or demonstrations. Those who were less dependent upon the government for their livelihood were more likely to participate in demonstrations.

"I participated in several of Dr. Martin Luther King's marches and in other demonstrations before them. This participation makes it difficult for me to achieve some of my goals today because of the change in political climate and the lack of committment of some white leaders to the goals of the civil rights movement."

-Member of Community Action Program

"I picketed Safeway stores to try to get black employees."
                                        -Musician

"Yes, at a Panther riot."

                                        -Music Teacher

The effectiveness of civil rights agitation has been questioned by some groups within the community. The respondents were questioned on their perceptions as to the achievement of civil rights goals. The following table reflects their views on this point.

Table 18

CIVIL RIGHTS GOALS

Reply to: "Do you feel the objectives of the Civil Rights movement have been achieved?"

	Traditional Elites (percent)	New Urban Elites (percent)
Achieved	43	34
Not achieved	43	57
No response	14	9
Total	100	100

It can be noted that a majority of the middle-class do not feel the Civil Rights movement accomplished its objectives. This is especially true of the new modernizing elites who generally felt the focus on the legal aspects of civil rights removed attention from economic inequality leaving the black community without a sound basis on which to build political power. They feel that dissent was suppressed without the fulfillment of many of the goals of the movement.

The Bouregoisie in Black Society

Increasingly blacks are defining their position in America as being a colonized one. The black bourgeoisie is no exception. In keeping with this colonial definition they see themselves as performing a needed function as intermediaries between the colonizers and the colonized. They emphasize that their actions are in the best interest of Afro-Americans and their obligations to the black community supercede other considerations. The new urban elites emphasize this point more strongly than the traditional elites.

The black bourgeoisie see themselves as leaders, intermediaries and a catalyst from which public opinion is built in the black community. The elites agree there is a gap widening between the middle-class and the lower-class but disagree when asked whether it is a deliberate colonizing technique. The traditional elites feel this division is deliberate but the new urban elites do not agree. Again, this may be a matter of perspective resulting from the different economic bases of the two groups.

The importance of a study of these two elites is immense in terms of public policy. There are considerable differences between the two groups although they are both dedicated to the betterment of black Americans. The manner in which this is done and priorities will depend to a great degree on the particular group that is dominate at a given time.

There is no evidence of an upper-class in the black community comparable to the upper-class in white society. However, there are a number of people who may be considered to have upper-class status within the framework of a colonized community. In terms of definition, in the community these people are part of the black bourgeoisie and some of their characteristics are consistent with E. Franklin Frazier's concept of the bouregoisie or the mijdle class as previously stated in this chapter. It has been established that the middle class considers themselves as intermediaries. The following is their definition of their relationship to the concept bourgeoisie.

Table 19

BLACK BOURGEOISIE, WEST

Reply to: "Do you think there is a black bourgeoisie in the West?"

	Traditional Elites (percent)	New Urban Elites (percent)
There is a black bourgeoisie	49	66
There is no black bourgeoisie	23	3
No response	28	31
Total	100	100

Table 20

BLACK BOURGEOISIE, OAKLAND

Reply to: "Is there a black bourgeoisie in this community?"

	Traditional Elites (percent	New Urban Elites (percent)
There is a black bourgeoisie	43	66
There is no black bourgeoisie	14	3
No response	43	31
Total	100	100

Selective employment supports the black middle class. It tends to widen the gap between those who have and the have nots. It is viewed by some as a means of breaking the cohesion of the community that is necessary to achieve common goals. This increasing gap is seen by some of the community residents as another means of social control. It leaves them in a quandry in that they must insist on the continued progress of those members of the black community.

Table 21

CLASS GAP

Reply to: "Dr. Andrew F. Brimmer indicates that the gap is widening between poor blacks and successful blacks, creating a new class division in the black community. Do you agree with this statement?"

	Traditional Elites (percent)	New Urban Elites (percent)
Agree	54	51
Disagree	29	26
No response	17	23
Total	100	100

Table 22

COLONIZING TECHNIQUES

Reply to: "It is believed by some that this is a deliberate colonizing technique. Do you agree or disagree?"

	Traditional Elites (percent)	New Urban Elites (percent)
Agree	54	34
Disagree	23	31
No response	23	35
Total	100	100

There are large differences of opinion between the two elite groups as regards to whether the gap being created within the race is a colonizing technique. The basis for these differences may be related to the manner in which the two groups achieved their economic and social positions. The traditionals usually achieved their positions through free enterprise and are more likely to accept an individualist posture of the capitalist tradition.

The dynamics of internal colonialism leads to colonized to be cynical of the advancement they receive as a result of their agitation. Their advances have a certain unreal quality to them because in reality they never expected to achieve the goals they fought hard to attain. It appears that the colonial system is contradictory in denying advancement on the basis of color on one hand and granting advancement on the other.

The importance of the black middle class in shaping community opinion is apparently a fact. This class controls the black press, church congregations, professional associations and have an influence in the educational process. Any sustained action on the part of the black community must gain the leadership and support of members of this class to be successful. Their impressions of the important issues facing the community and how they are to be overcome are critical for public policy.

Actions to achieve equality by the black community in the immediate future will revolve around better employment, housing, education and increased intra-community political activity. Whereas all of the goals of the civil rights movement were not achieved in terms of a complete modernization of the political process the emphasis of activism will probably be on economic issues. At least it can be expected the black elites will tend to move in this direction. It can be expected that the central focus of activity will be through economic and political processes where there has been significant gains in the recent past. It is apparent the decrease in civil rights activity in terms of street demonstrations is a result of a change in tactics by the black middle-class who lead most of the significant demonstrations in the 1960's. This study indicates the two elite groups may agree on many issues but they disagree on others with varying degrees of intensity.

Conclusion

The data indicates there is very little in terms of general ideological differences between the new urban elites and the traditional black middle-class in the area of race relations. The ideology is essentially integrationist but their frustrations with American society has angered some who indicate a preference for autonomy in some situations. On the other hand, there is a minority that is somewhat separatist. The size of this minority depends upon the particular issue and the particular situation in an institutional area.

In the context of this analysis it is important to note a majority (57%) of the new elites feel blacks are moving toward integration and only (14%) of the traditional elites feel Afro-Americans are moving in that direction. The perception of a slow rate of improvement for blacks, sixty percent for both elite groups provides fertile ground for separatist agitation.

The elites are almost evenly divided on the concept of internal colonization and a substantial majority rejects the notion of black nationalism. The data does not indicate the black middle-class feel a complete sense of powerlessness or impotency.

There is apparently a sense of faith in the American people or the elites' ability to cope with racial problems within the system that is generally ignored in militant rhetoric. In response to whether Afro-Americans are likely to be exterminated and not assimilated, there was a majority who replied in the negative. A large majority not only supports integration but believes it is possible. This is not a blind allegiance to melting pot theory of race relations. The elites in both groups indicate for various reasons their obligations to the black community supercedes any obligations to the American society as a whole. In defining their situation they perceive integration is in the best interest of the society as a whole and the black community. Given this definition, integration is the logical and reasonable way to proceed in alleviating racial tensions and bring about equality of opportunity.

It is clear, the black middle-class became a significant force in terms of social change in the black community in the 1960's. Contrary to general impressions in the white community, black agitation for social change in the black community in the 1960's. Contrary to general impressions in the white community, black agitation for social change and civil rights were largely led by this responsible class. In areas where they did not lead, they supported the objectives if not the tactics of other militants. There is no information that indicates their goals or objectives are significantly different from those of the black lower classes.

The black middle-class in Oakland is aware that all of the goals of the civil rights movement of the 1960's have not been achieved but they take well deserved pride in the accomplishments gained in the fields of politics, administration and public accommodations. They are disappointed as to the lack of progress in areas of economics, jobs, elimination of poverty, education and social integration. Modernization in the latter areas has not proceeded apace with other improvements in the community and it is in this area emphasis will be focused in the future.

The cultural aspects of the social upheavals of the 1960's had a serious impact upon this group. The black youth played an important part in revising a trend toward cultural assimilation. Middle-class youth openly questioned the notion of the superiority of white American cultural values and actively rebelled against being absorbed into a large American melting pot that denied them a sense of identity. The youth led the battle to change the curriculums at various educational institutions to make them more relevant to their emerging sense of awareness. These changes not only brought about increased appreciation for black history, art and music, they also increased pride within the black community in some cases liberating the middle class from their close identity with the colonizer.

The black middle-class refuse to accept the notion of cooptation that is often implied with the roles of intermediaries. This group of leaders accepts the responsibility and obligations of the leadership role. They do not view the role of intermediary as being anti-ethical to the progress of blacks. On the contrary, they view their role as being one of experts representing the interest of oppressed people to the power structure and use themselves working in the interest of the black masses. They see their roles as not only spokesmen and representatives, but in a more positive light. They feel an obligation to lead and teach in a continued effort to modernize and politicize the black community. Very often they are in the vanguard of agitation for employment, employment training, redevelopment funds to upgrade housing and better educational opportunities. Although, they are often criticized by both the black lower-classes and the white community for lack of leadership, little progress would have been made in race relations without the cooperation of this group.

Criticism from the lower classes can be expected because in a modernizing society all segments of the community do not achieve at the same rates. As Arthur Brimmer has indicated, the gap between the lower classes and the middle class is widening in view of the increased education and employability of some blacks in the community. Programs for improvement of the poor simply have not been designed to bring all of them into the mainstream of America's economic and social life. However, some of the criticism of the middle class by these lower on the socio-economic ladder is brought about by the actions of the middle-class.

The National Association of Negro Business and Professional Women's Clubs Incorporated lists twenty-nine political clubs, twenty-one cultural organizations, one hundred eighty-five social clubs, twenty-nine business and professional organizations, thirty-one fraternity and sorority chapters and thirty other fraternal organizations as being active in the East Bay area of California among the black middle-class. This tendency to organize into exclusive groups tends to alienate the lower classes who view these elite organizations with a great deal of suspicion because they are usually excluded from membership in them. Certainly, these groups form the core of leadership of the black community and the black masses are eliminated from participation directly in the decision making process within the community. In some instances, black grassroots militant organizations have capitalized on this situation and have risen to present the viewpoints of the alienated on matters affecting them directly.

Both the traditional and new urban elites agree the black community is becoming more stratified in regards to economic class but they differ on whether it is a deliberate action on the part of the American society. In general, they feel this division can be minimized through responsible leadership on their part and with improvements in the areas of education and job opportunities.

One of the principle methods of modernizing black masses is through conspicuous consumption of the middle class. This method has differential effects on the lower classes. In some instances, this method will achieve a degree of success but in others the gap between the goals of a modern society and the ligitimized means of achieving those goals are too great to overcome. Often this may lead to additional frustration on the part of the lower classes that may manifest itself in anti-social behavior or the total rejection of the cultural goals of the middle-class. There is evidence of this occurring in Oakland where large segments of the lower class no longer strive to achieve middle-class goals. Instead they turn inwardly to those who are similarly situated to gain the social approval that is necessary to justify their existence. It is in this area the black middle-class fails although there is no lack of concern or devotion on their part to the achievement of black aspirations.

A member of a prominent black church in Oakland was highly critical of the special Sunday services held annually for black sororities in the area. His bitterness was directed at the elitist aspect of the service and he wondered why there were no special services for the laborers, manual workers, welfare mothers and others who were the stalwarts of the church, attending services regularly and contributing continually to the financial viability of the church. He was resentful of the use of the church on a given day by people who showed very little interest in it on other occasions and who drove to the services in large fine automobiles and expensive dress much as a person would, going to a formal outing. He felt the positive aspects of religious worship was perverted on these occasions.

A parent indicated her disgust with the Links Cotillion's debutante ball, one of the larger social events by black society in the Bay area. She felt the ball was not related to anything relevant to the community. She resented the exclusiveness of the faffir. It is apparent that only those with considerable means can afford this event.

There has been a great deal of resentment directed toward the black middle-class in many areas that are the results of their tendency to join exclusive social organizations. As the number of clubs and organizations indicates, black elites in the Bay Area are a highly organized group of people. They are in a position to award social and political approval to various segments of the black community and when the lower classes are denied access to this means of approval, they will find others that circumvent the middle class. To the extent the lower classes are able to find an alternative means of gaining social approval the ability of the middle-class to lead or fulfill its traditional role as intermediaries is inhibited.

It is important in terms of public policy to understand that all classes of the black community in Oakland are aware of the internal colonial aspects of the community and injustices perpetuated on one segment of the community tend to have an integrationist effect on the entire black community. The gap between classes, notwithstanding, the community pulls together in the same manner as nations do when there is a foreign threat to its national interest. It is imperative to understand that in spite of the class differences, the black community is united in its opposition to racial oppression.

BIBLIOGRAPHY

1. Collected works, newspapers and other primary sources.

American College Dictionary (New York: Random House Publishers, 1967)

Moore, Percy, Curt Aller and Richard R. Kern, The Press and the OEDCI, 1969-1971 (The Oakland Economic Development Council, Inc., 1971)

Oakland Newsletter, City in Trouble, Vol. 1, No. 1, June 8, 1970

Pressman, Jeffrey, Proconditions of Mayoral Leadership (Paper prepared for a meeting of the American Political Science Association, September 1970, Los Angeles, California)

Society (Vol. 9, No. 10, October 1972)

Tamaki, Donald K., Oakland Politics and Powerless Pressure Groups (Unpublished paper, University of California, 1970)

The Oakland Tribune, June 29, 1972, p. 22, col. 4

The Oakland Independent, December 19, 1929

The Oakland Independent, May 30, 1910

The Oakland Sunshine, December 21, 1907

The Oakland Sunshine, September 11, 1909

The Oakland Sunshine, August 7, 1915

The Oakland Sunshine, August 18, 1915

The Oakland Sunshine, July 24, 1915

The Oakland Sunshine, December 27, 1913

The New York Times, July 7, 1971

The New York Times , July 8, 1971

The New York Times, March 10, 1960

The New York Times , July 9, 1972

The New York Times, May 10, 1960

The New York Times, July 9, 1971

The San Francisco Chronicle, July 13, 1972

United States Census, U.S. Department of Commerce, Bureau of Census Consumer Income, July 1973

United States Department of Commerce, The Social and Economic Status of the
Black Population, Current Reports, July 1973

2. Theoretical and historical sources.

Apter, David E., Some Conceptual Approaches to the Study of Modernization,
Englewood Cliffs: Prentice-Hall, Inc., 1968

Apter, David E., The Politics of Modernization, Chicago: University of Chicago
Press, 1965

Apter, David E., Ghana in Transition, New York: Antheneum, 1963

Apter, David E., The Political Kingdom in Uganda, Princeton: Princeton University Press, 1961

Bennett, Lerone Jr., Black Bourgeoisie Revisited, Ebony, Vol. XXVIII, No. 10,
August 1973

Bennett, Lerone Jr., The Quest for Economic Security, Ebony, February 1974

Black, Cyril E., The Dynamics of Modernization, New York: Harper and Row,
Publishers, 1966

Blauner, Robert, Racial Oppression in America, New York: Harper and Row,
Publishers, 1972

Blauner, Robert, Internal Colonialism and Ghetto Revolt, Social Problems, Vol.
16, No. 4, Spring 1969

Carmichael, Stokley and Charles Hamilton, Black Power, New York: Random House,
1967

Cliffe, Lionel, ed., One Party Democracy, Nairobi, Kenya: East African Publishing House, 1965

Coleman, James S., The Politics of Sub-Saharan Africa, in Gabriel A. Almond and
James S. Coleman, The Politics of Developing Areas, Princeton: Princeton
University Press, 1960

Cushman, Robert F., Cases in Civil Liberties, New York: Appleton-Century-Crofts,
1968

Deutsch, Karl, Social Mobilization and Political Development, Wilbert E. Moore
and Neil J. Smelser Eds., Modernization of Traditional Societies, Englewood Cliffs: Prentice Hall, Inc., 1966

Drake, St. Clair and Horace R. Cayton, Black Metropolis, Vol. II, New York:
Harcourt, Brace and World, Inc., 1962

DuBois, William E. B., Black Reconstruction, New York: Russell and Russell, 1962

Eisenstadt, S. N., "Initial Institutional Patterns of Political Modernization"
in Claude E. Welch, Jr., Political Modernization, Belmont, California:
Wadsworth Publishing Co., Inc., Belmont, California, 1967

Eisenstadt, S. N., Modernization: Protest and Change, Englewood Cliffs, New
    Jersey: Prentice-Hall, 1968

Eisenstadt, S. N., "Bureaucracy and Political Development" in Joseph LaPalomara,
    Bureaucracy and Political Development, Princeton: Princeton University
    Press, 1967

Elkins, Stanley M., Slavery, Chicago: University of Chicago Press, 1968

Fanon, Frantz, The Wretched of the Earth, New York: Grove Press, 1967

Fanon, Frantz, Black Skins White Masks, New York: Grove Press, 1967

Farley, Reynolds, "Changing Distribution of Negroes Within Metropolitan Areas,"
    American Journal of Sociology, Vol. 75, No. 4, January 1970

Feuer, Lewis S., ed., Marx and Engels, Garden City: Doubleday and Company,
    Inc., 1959

Franklin, John H., From Slavery to Freedom, New York: Alfred A. Knopf, 1967

Friedland, William H., A Sociological Approach to Modernization, Ithaca: Cornell
    University Press, 1969

Frazier, E. Franklin, The Negro in the United States, New York: MacMillan Press,
    1958

Frazier, E. Franklin, Black Bourgeoisie, London: Collier-MacMillan, 1957

Frazier, E. Franklin, The Negro Church, New York: Antheneum Press, 1948

Genovese, Eugene D., "An Encounter on the Origins of Black Nationalism," in
    Black Liberation Politics ed. Edward Greer, Boston: Allyn and Bacon, Inc.,
    1971

Germani, Gino, Secularization, Modernization and Economic Development in the
    Protestant Ethnic Modernization, ed. S. N. Eisenstadt, New York: Basic
    Books, Inc., Publishers, 1968

Hayes, Edward C., Power Structure and Urban Policy: Who Rules in Oakland?,
    New York: McGraw-Hill Book Company, 1972

Hermalin, Albert I. and Reynold Farley, "Potential for Residential Integration
    in Cities and Suburbs: Implications for Busing Controversy," American
    Sociological Review, July 1973

Huntington, S. P., "Political Development and Political Decay" in Claude E.
    Welch, Jr., Political Modernization, Belmont, California: Wadsworth
    Publishers, 1967

Inkeles, Alex, "The Modernization of Man," in Modernization: The Dynamics of
    Growth, ed. Myron Weiner, New York: Basic Books, Inc., 1966

Jordan, Winthrop, White Over Black, Baltimore: Penguin Books, Inc., 1969

Katz, William L., Eyewitness: The Negro in American History, New York: Nitsan Publishing Corporation, 1968

Kelly, Alfred H. and Winifred A. Harbison, The American Constitution, Its Origin and Development, New York: W. W. Norton and Company, 1963

Kilson, Martin, Political Change in a West African State, Cambridge: Harvard University Press, 1966

LeVine, Victor T., Political Leadership in Africa, Palo Alto: The Hoover Institute on War, Revolution and Race, Stanford University, 1967

McPherson, James Alan, "The Story of the Contract Buyers League," The Atlantic, Vol. 229, No. 4, April 1972

McWilliams, Carey, North from Mexico, New York: Greenwood Press , Publishers, 1968

Memmi, Albert, The Colonizer and the Colonized, Boston: Beacon Press, 1965

Marx, Gary T., Protest and Prejudice, New York: Harper and Row Publishers, 1967

Poinsett, Alex, "Class Patterns in Black Politics" Ebony, Vol. XXVIII, No. 10, August 1973

Reiseman, Leonard, "Social Stratification" in Sociology: an Introduction, ed. Neil Smelser, New York: John Wiley and Sons, 1973

Silberman, Crises in Black and White, New York: Random House, 1968

Stampp, Kenneth M., The Peculiar Institution, New York: Knopf, 1956

Tannenbaum, Frank, Slave and Citizen, New York: Vintage Books, 1946

Wallerstein, Immanuel, Africa: The Politics of Independence, Vintage Books, New York, 1961

Willhelm, Sidney, Who Needs the Negro?, New York: Anchor Books, 1971

Wilson, James Z., "Two Negro Politicians: An Interpretation," Midwest Journal of Political Science, Vol. IV, November 1966

Zolberg, Aristide R., "Mass Parties and National Integration: The Case of the Ivory Coast," The Journal of Politics, Vol. 25, No. 1, February 1963

Zolbert, Aristide R., One-Party Government in the Ivory Coast, Princeton: Princeton University Press, 1969